Can we believe Genesis today?

Ernest Lucas

Can we believe Genesis today?

The Bible and the questions of science

Inter-Varsity Press

INTER-VARSITY PRESS
Norton Street, Nottingham NG7 3HR, England
Email: ivp@ivpbooks.com
Website: www.ivpbooks.com

First edition published under the title Genesis Today *by Scripture Union in 1989. Reissued by Christian Impact in 1995.*

Second edition 2001
Third edition 2005
Reprinted 2007

British Library Cataloguing in Publication Data
A catalogue record for this book is available from the British Library.

ISBN-10: 1-84474-120-6
ISBN-13: 978-1-84474-120-5

Set in Garamond
Typeset in Great Britain
Printed and bound by Creative Print & Design (Wales) Ltd, Ebbw Vale

Inter-Varsity Press publishes Christian books that are true to the Bible and that communicate the gospel, develop discipleship and strengthen the church for its mission in the world.

Inter-Varsity Press is closely linked with the Universities and Colleges Christian Fellowship, a student movement connecting Christian Unions in universities and colleges throughout Great Britain, and a member movement of the International Fellowship of Evangelical Students.
Website: www.uccf.org.uk

Contents

Acknowledgments

This book has been a number of years in the making. I want to express my thanks to all those who have helped me to write it.

It is impossible to mention everyone who helped me develop my thinking about science and Christianity in general, and about science and Genesis in particular – by their lectures, books, letters and personal conversations. Many of these have been members of The American Scientific Affiliation, Christians in Science (formerly The Research Scientists' Christian Fellowship), The Creation Research Society and The Tyndale Fellowship for Biblical Research. They, of course, are not to be held responsible for my conclusions. Some would certainly not accept particular ones.

Thanks are due to Beck Totterdell of SU Publishing for her editorial help in producing the first edition of this book, to Colin Duriez of IVP for his encouragement and help in producing this revised edition, and to Marie

Can we believe Genesis today?

Palmer of IVP, who put the text of the first edition on to computer disk ready for revision because the original disks had gone astray.

Above all, I want to thank my wife Hazel and our sons Craig and Stuart for their encouragement and support while I was writing this book, despite the hours it took out of our time together as a family.

Preface

Since the writing of the first edition of this book (*Genesis Today*, published in 1989), science has moved on in many of the areas that were touched on. There have also been some important developments in the Christian debate about the issues dealt with. The fact that two printings of the book had sold out, and that people were still contacting bookshops (and me) wanting to buy it, encouraged me to believe that it would be worth producing a new edition. I am grateful to IVP for their willingness to publish it.

In this revised and enlarged edition, changes have therefore been made throughout, but the most notable change is the addition of a new chapter (ch. 6). The character of the book has not been changed, however. It is still intended very much to be an introduction to understanding Genesis 1 – 11 in the light of modern scientific discoveries and ideas. It seeks to give a fair presentation of different Christian positions on the issues

Can we believe Genesis today?

referred to, but inevitably my own conclusions are stated from time to time.

Ernest Lucas
2000

Start here ...

When we read the Bible we usually do so with all kinds of ideas and questions buzzing around in our minds. This is especially so if the passage we are reading is one that we know to be difficult or controversial, like Genesis 1 – 11, which we will study in some detail. These ideas and questions can be a hindrance to understanding what we read. They can act like a fog, preventing us seeing things clearly and confusing us so that we go down the wrong paths. That is why this book does not start by going straight to Genesis 1:1 and asking, 'What does it mean?' Instead, we begin with some fog-dispersal. It will take some time, but the result will be worth it when we turn our attention to Genesis 1 – 11.

This book is about Genesis and how far scientific discoveries can help us to understand it. Many people have only the vaguest ideas about what science is and about what it can and cannot tell us. This is true even of some scientists! Few have a clear idea of the nature of scientific theories and laws and how they are related. Yet the arguments that surround Genesis are full of references to such things as the *theory* of evolution and the second *law* of thermodynamics. So we must spend some time dispersing the fog that surrounds science in many people's minds. I will do this as clearly and simply as possible without over-simplifying. None of this will require you to have much knowledge of science, just a willingness to think about what you read!

Some people are confused about the nature of the Bible, how it should be interpreted, and what we can and cannot expect it to tell us. Here, too, some fog-dispersal is needed. Even if you have been a reader of the Bible for some time, you should find this a useful refresher course on understanding the Bible. It will equip you to look more carefully at those chapters about whose interpretation there is some disagreement.

It would be foolish and arrogant to claim that this book will solve all the problems of Genesis 1 – 11 for you. What I hope it will do is present clearly the different interpretations held by Bible-believing Christians, and the strengths and weaknesses of those interpretations. Inevitably, my own preferences will become clear. However, the aim is that by the end of the book you will be better able to come to your own conclusions on the basis of a clearer understanding of the alternatives.

So, if you are sitting comfortably, we will begin …

1

Looking for truth

It was a warm summer evening. Two people were walking along the beach, listening to the gentle lapping of the waves and looking at the star-studded sky. They both spotted a light flashing out at sea.

One of them, a retired physicist, was the kind of scientist who thought of nothing but his work. Science was his life. He rushed to his car where, being the sort of person he was, he kept all kinds of scientific equipment. He got out a stop watch and timed the flashes. He got out a photometer and measured the brightness of the flashes. He set up a spectrometer and recorded their spectrum. He noted the position of the light against the background stars. As he drove home along the coast road, he stopped a couple of times and noted its position again, doing some triangulation calculations. When he got home his wife said, 'You look excited, dear! Did you see something interesting tonight?' 'Yes,' he said, 'I saw what I deduced was a heated tungsten filament, enclosed in a silica

13

envelope, emitting a regular pattern of flashes of visible radiation at an intensity of 2,500 lumens from a distance of about 850 metres offshore.'

The other person on the beach that night was a teenager going home from Sea Scouts. When he got home his mother said, 'You look excited dear, did you see something interesting tonight?' 'Yes,' he said, 'I saw a boat signalling SOS, and I telephoned the coastguard, and they sent out the lifeboat.'

Which of these two people gave the more accurate description of what they both saw? Neither. They each gave a perfectly accurate description but in quite different terms. The physicist described it in the only way it could be described within the bounds of the language, concepts and quantities recognized in physics. For him to have said more would have been to become 'unscientific', in the sense of going beyond what a physicist could say purely as a physicist. Physics can measure and talk about flashes of light; it knows nothing of Morse code and SOS. Such things belong to a different area of human experience.

The limitations of science

What this imaginary story illustrates is that physics, and indeed all science, has its limits. It works with carefully defined, and therefore strictly limited, methods and concepts. These restrict the kind of questions that scientists can ask and answer while using a scientific approach. Scientists are concerned with the physical world of matter and energy. They limit themselves to what can be counted, weighed and measured. As far as possible they try to express their findings in terms of mathematical equations. In other words, science is concerned with how the physical world works – its mechanism. Truly scientific

14

questions can always be expressed as 'How?' questions. The physicist in our story was answering the question, 'How were the flashes of light being produced?'

There are, however, many other types of question that we want to ask. In some situations they are much more important than the 'How?' questions. For the people actually in the boat out at sea, it was much more important that the Sea Scout asked, 'Why is somebody flashing a light?' and 'What do the flashes mean?' Fortunately for them, he could read the message and understand its meaning because he knew Morse code, even though he may have known little physics.

By itself science can never answer questions of meaning – the 'Why?' questions. Scientific attempts to answer them always end up as 'How?' answers. Suppose a medical doctor were asked, 'Why did Captain Oates die on the way back from the South Pole with Captain Scott?' He could only give a definite answer if he could find the body and carry out a post-mortem examination. Then he would no doubt say, in the correct medical terminology, that he died of extreme cold, frostbite and the other effects of exposure to the Antarctic weather, which caused his body to stop functioning. That is really a mechanistic 'how'-type answer: how the Antarctic conditions affected his body with the result that he died. It says nothing about the meaning of this death in human and moral terms: an act of self-sacrifice in an attempt to free his friends of the hindrance of a sick man, in the hope that they could then travel faster and reach base camp before their resources ran out.

Many of the problems people have regarding science and the Bible result from the failure, or refusal, to understand the limitations of science. We live in a culture that has been affected deeply by 300 years of largely successful scientific endeavour. Among other things, it has affected the popular idea of truth. During most of the twentieth century, for most people scientific knowledge was seen as *the truth*. There are a number of reasons for this: the success of science, the preciseness of most scientific explanations, the fact that (usually) scientists can agree about their answers whilst other people (e.g. politicians, economists, theologians) cannot agree. These and other reasons gave scientific truth considerable prestige.

During the last two decades of the century, scientific truth lost some of its prestige. This was partly because some highly publicized problems, such as BSE in beef cattle, showed that scientists do not always agree and cannot always provide a ready solution. There has also been the rise of a growing challenge to the dominance of the rationalistic thinking that has been a characteristic of western culture since the Enlightenment of the eighteenth century. This is part of the complex phenomenon that has come to be called 'postmodernism'. Despite this shift, it is still the case that most people regard scientific knowledge as the most reliable form of truth. The relative prestige still given to scientific truth supports two widely held assumptions.

The first is that, in areas of human experience that are not open to scientific study, especially morality and religion, truth is either purely relative ('if it makes you happy that's fine, but don't force your view on me') or non-existent. The public debate about Aids gives evidence of this. It has centred on 'safe sex', how to avoid getting Aids, but it has ignored discussing what forms of sexual activity are *morally* right or wrong – because there is no widely accepted basis for making such moral decisions. Science is looked to for a purely practical solution to the problem, such as a vaccine against Aids.

Secondly, anyone or anything that seems to question, or disagree with, current scientific ideas is regarded with suspicion or discounted as wrong. Since the Bible seems at odds with modern scientific ideas in some places, especially the early chapters of Genesis, it is ignored or rejected as being out of date.

If we can see the limitations of science, we can see that these assumptions are wrong and therefore harmful. The methods and terms of reference of science prevent it from investigating questions of value and meaning, the questions with which morality and religion claim to deal. But this does not mean that questions about value and meaning are not worth asking. Nor does it follow that there are no moral or religious truths. What it does show is that in these areas truth has to be reached by other means.

Limited in providing values

How valuable is a human being? Apparently most people think humans have some value because they think that murder is wrong. The law says that it is wrong to kill a person but not wrong to kill and eat a chicken. How can a scientist put a value on a human being?

A chemist might analyse a human body in terms of its chemical constituents. However, to 'value' it one would have to bring in the external, non-scientific criterion of the market value of the chemicals. This would put a premium on those with gold fillings in their teeth!

A zoologist might think in terms of humans as being one of the most recent products of the process of the evolution of life on earth. But why should the most recent product be the most highly valued? Why not put most value on, say, the species that has been around longest? At least it has shown staying power! We might be tempted to value humans in terms of the size of their brains in relation to body size. But why choose that criterion instead of, say, running speed? The best the zoologist can do is to rank humans alongside other life forms in terms of certain characteristics; we have to go outside of science in order to put any value or moral significance on these characteristics.

A social scientist might try to argue that murder is 'wrong' because it destabilizes and disrupts society. But why should it be 'good' to have a stable society? A moral position is being assumed here without its being argued for on any scientific grounds. We might argue that it is 'convenient' (perhaps in financial terms) to kill the victim. Whose convenience is to be given preference?

Moral philosophers have, of course, discussed questions like this at great length. The great majority would agree that science (the study of 'what is', the way things are) cannot serve as a basis for deciding moral values ('what should be', the way things ought to be done). Questions of value have to be decided on other grounds. Some atheistic philosophers even admit that, if there is no God, there are no rational, universal grounds for morality or meaning. The influential philosopher Jean-Paul Sartre wrote,

> The [atheistic] existentialist finds it extremely embarrassing that God does not exist, for there disappears with him all possibility of finding values in an intelligible heaven (*Existentialism and Humanism* [London: Methuen, 1973], p. 33).

Sartre's reference to the 'intelligibility' or meaningfulness of life brings us to the other major limitation of science. It cannot answer questions such as, 'What is life all about? Is there any meaning to it all?'

Limited in giving meaning

Our belief that there is meaning to life is closely linked to our reasoning ability, and so with rationality. But why should we trust our minds, or indeed those of the scientists whose conclusions we accept as 'reliable knowledge'? Is there any scientific basis for this trust? The simple answer is, no.

The most that science can do is tell us how our brains work: the physics and chemistry of what goes on in our brain cells. Science cannot tell us the meaning of these physical and chemical happenings in terms of reason and logic. We are back to our story. The physicist could say how the flashes of light were produced but nothing about the message they carried.

Some people have argued that if our thought processes can be explained in terms of physics and chemistry, and so in terms of apparently fixed laws of nature, then our thoughts are completely determined by these laws. There is no such thing as free will. When Professor Taylor, a mathematician at London University, argued this way in *New Scientist* magazine in 1971, he received this riposte in the letters column from one of the magazine's readers:

Prof. Taylor's resolved our confusion
and proved that free will's a delusion.
But though he has said it
He can't expect credit,
Since he's programmed to draw this conclusion.

If the scientific explanation of our thought processes is

the only one, then Professor Taylor is right and our thoughts are completely determined. The reader is also right: we have no grounds for believing or accepting what other people say. They have to believe what they do, and if it differs from what I believe, there is no way of resolving the difference – it is rooted in the physics and chemistry of our brains, not in logic. The eminent biologist Professor J. B. S. Haldane recognized this a long time ago, when he wrote:

> If my mental processes are determined wholly by the atoms in my brain I have no reason to suppose that my beliefs are true. They may be sound chemically, but that does not make them sound logically. And hence I have no reason for supposing my brain to be composed of atoms. In order to escape from this necessity of sawing away the branch on which I am sitting, so to speak, I am compelled to believe that mind is not wholly conditioned by matter (*Possible Worlds* [London: Chatto & Windus, 1932], p. 209).

Haldane went on to say that it is necessary to believe in an 'infinite mind' existing 'behind nature' in order to explain the existence of human rationality.

A child of Christianity

Here, then, we can see that logic and reason, which are fundamental to the whole scientific enterprise, cannot be explained or proved reliable by science itself. Their value has to be assumed by scientists. But on what grounds? Historically, the answer to that question is quite clear. The founders of modern science believed in reason and in its ability to understand nature on thoroughly Christian grounds. In fact one philosopher, Professor J. MacMurray, has claimed that 'Science is the legitimate child of a great religious movement, and its genealogy goes back to Jesus' (*Reason and Emotion*, p. 172). This may seem a strange thing to say today, when many people have the impression that science and Christianity are to some extent rivals. However, historians and philosophers of science since the middle of the last century have made it increasingly clear that, among the various factors that contributed to the rise of modern science, the Christian beliefs that were widely held in late medieval Europe played an important part.

Of all the great civilizations that the world has known, why was it that modern science was born in Christian Europe towards the end of the Middle Ages? The knowledge about the world and the technical expertise possessed in other cultures were not in themselves enough to get science going, as we know it. The Greeks, the Hindus of the Ganges valley, the Arabs and others had considerable knowledge and technical expertise, but they never developed science as an ongoing movement. What was missing was the right framework of thought that would give people the confidence and motivation to allow scientific study to flourish. This was provided by Christianity. This is why a leading historian of science says:

> The scientific quest found fertile soil only when faith in a personal, rational Creator had truly permeated a whole culture, beginning with the centuries of the High Middle Ages. It was that faith which provided in sufficient measure, confidence in the rationality of the universe, trust in progress, and appreciation of the qualitative method, all

indispensable ingredients of the scientific quest
(Jaki, *Science and Creation*, p. viii).

More recently, writing from the perspective of an expert
in comparative religion and the history of religion, Harold
Turner has argued that the Judeo-Christian view of nature
was an 'essential but not sufficient cause' of the rise of
modern science (*The Roots of Science*, p. 171). He quotes
with approval the conclusion of Lloyd Geering:

> ... there is a direct correlation between the de-
> sacralization of the natural world and the rise of the
> modern scientific enterprise. Modern science
> evolved in the Western world instead of elsewhere
> as an indirect consequence of Christian culture
> (*Tomorrow's God* [Wellington, NZ: Bridget Wil-
> liams Books, 1994], p. 115).

The 'de-sacralization' of the world spoken of here, which
means not treating it as divine or even semi-divine, arises
from the biblical understanding of how the world is
related to God.

The Bible teaches that the world was created by God
out of nothing as an act of his free will (Hebrews 11:3). It
depends on him for its continued existence moment by
moment (Hebrews 1:3). Since God acted as a free agent
and since we cannot presume to be able to predict what he
would have done, the only way we can find out about and
understand his creation is by studying it through
observation and experiment.

The God of the Bible is a personal, rational and faithful
Creator. Therefore his creation can be expected to be
orderly and rational. Passages such as Genesis 1 and 8:22
support this conclusion. It was on this basis that the early

scientists developed the concept of natural laws and began to look for them.

According to Genesis 1:26–27 human beings are made in the image and likeness of God. This gave the early scientists confidence to believe that their minds were finite reflections of God's mind and that they would therefore be able to understand his creation and his natural laws. They did have grounds for relying on human reason and logic.

The command of Genesis 1:28 to rule over the earth, and of Genesis 2:15 to take care of the garden of Eden, gave a religious motivation for scientific study of nature. It was seen as a way of carrying out these commands. Indeed, it was seen by some as a way of co-operating with God to repair some of the damage done to nature by the disobedience of Adam and Eve.

Of course, only a minority of scientists today understand or accept this Christian framework for what they are doing. That is one reason why there is considerable debate amongst philosophers of science about the nature and basis of scientific truth. The fact is that originally the scientific enterprise found its purpose and meaning outside of itself, in Christian theology. Today, with that purpose and meaning largely neglected, it is not possible to find any other widely acceptable basis for science.

Conclusions

Three things become clear from this look at the nature of scientific truth, its limitations and its basis.

Science cannot explain everything

Firstly, the person who is sceptical about Christianity and tempted to believe that science provides the explanation for everything should be more cautious. We have seen that that belief is at best muddle-headed and at worst self-defeating.

It is a muddle-headed belief because it fails to recognize the self-imposed limitations of science and therefore the wide range of questions which science cannot answer. These questions are worth serious exploration by non-scientific means before they are written off as pointless. After all, down the centuries many people have found the answers to them to be of more importance than scientific knowledge!

It is a self-defeating belief if, recognizing the limits of science, it still insists that scientific truth is *the* truth. We have seen that this insistence undermines all belief in rationality and so undermines science itself.

Science explores God's truth

Secondly, Christians who are suspicious about, even afraid of, science should be encouraged to take a more positive attitude to it. Although, like the general population in the West, the majority of scientists today are not Christians, modern science is to some extent 'a child of Christianity' and there is nothing inherently anti-Christian about it. In fact, to some extent we can point to the success of science as evidence of the truth of the Christian beliefs upon which it was founded. When Christianity is attacked in the name of science, it is usually being attacked on grounds that are not purely scientific. Generally, an anti-Christian philosophy lies behind the scientific jargon, with scientific facts being brought in to make the argument sound scientific. Christians have nothing to fear from facing up to the established findings of science, because they are facts about God's creation. As such, they will eventually fit into the overall picture of his truth.

Of course, it is not always easy to distinguish between the 'established findings' of science and those that are more provisional. Upheavals in thought over the last one hundred years – relativity and quantum mechanics in physics and plate tectonics in geology, for instance – have taught scientists the danger of presumption and the need for open-minded humility. Some have not learnt the lessons very well! We will return in the next chapter to this question of how much reliance we can put on particular scientific findings and theories.

God the Creator is still necessary

Thirdly, we need to look at one particular area in which the limitations of the scientific approach are obvious. Modern science contains theories about the origin of the universe, the origin of the solar system and, of course, the origin of life on earth. All these are expressed in purely materialistic terms without any reference to God, so does this mean that scientists have shown that a creator God is unnecessary? Some scientists who are atheists claim that they have. However, they are forgetting the limitations of science and claiming too much. The most that a scientist can claim for a theory about the origin of the universe, for example, is that it explains *how* God, if he exists, brought the universe into being – what mechanism he used. It certainly does not explain away the need for the God of the Bible. Christians believe in a God who thought up and brought into being matter, energy and time and the fundamental laws and forces of nature which govern their behaviour. Moreover, he continues to keep them in being. He was free to bring the universe into being by whatever process he chose, and the scientist is free to study the universe to see if that process can be discovered and understood.

Similarly, it is possible that God chose to bring all or some life forms into being through what biologists call the process of evolution. It would not make him any less the creator if he did so. An engineer, for example, could design and build a robot that could then design and build an even more complex robot. Could not the engineer legitimately claim to be the inventor of the more complex robot? Archbishop Frederick Temple was questioned about the implications of the theory of evolution when it was still quite novel. He reportedly replied, 'We used to believe in a God who made things. Now we must believe in a God who made things make themselves.' He could not see that this was any challenge to belief in a creator. Which God is in fact the more awesome – one who just makes things or one who can make things make themselves?

Facing up to apparent clashes

At this point some Christians might be feeling a bit unhappy. Surely the Bible tells us *how* God created the heavens and the earth and all living things? And doesn't it tell a rather different story from that told by modern science? Answers to these questions are going to take up the major part of this book. So here we will simply mention that, when there is an apparent clash between science and the Bible, at least three possible conclusions could be drawn:

1. *The Bible might be right and the scientists wrong.* Scientific theories do come and go, and occasionally there are radical changes in scientific views. Christians should not be slavish followers of scientific fashion. It is important that Christians in science should be prepared to

ask radical questions about accepted scientific orthodoxy and should oppose scientific arrogance and prejudice, provided they do this in a truly scientific way.

2. *The scientists might be right and the Bible wrong.* Some Christians have taken this view with regard to the early chapters of Genesis and so have had to give up the traditional Christian doctrine of the Bible as God's Word. Those who believe that the Bible is indeed the inspired word of the creator, whose glory is revealed in nature, will never regard this as a necessary option. Ultimately it must be possible to harmonize scientific truth and biblical teaching.

3. *The scientists might be right and our interpretation of the Bible might be wrong.* Just as scientists need humility, so do Christians! However traditional and cherished our particular understanding of a Bible passage may be, it is still only our interpretation of it and it might be mistaken. If the scientists show us that it is mistaken, then we should be grateful to them for helping us to take a step nearer to a true understanding of God's Word.

Further reading

J. H. Brooke, *Science and Religion: Some historical perspectives* (Cambridge: CUP, 1991). A detailed study of the sometimes complex relationship between scientific thought and religious belief.

S. L. Jaki, *Science and Creation* (Edinburgh: Scottish Academic Press, 1974). A detailed study of the history of science that concentrates on how the religious beliefs in different cultures helped or hindered its development.

J. MacMurray, *Reason and Emotion* (London: Faber & Faber, 1962). Contains an essay on 'Science and religion', from which the quotation in this chapter is taken.

C. A. Russell, *Cross-currents: Interactions between science and faith* (Leicester: IVP, 1985). A very readable account of the history of science.

H. Turner, *The Roots of Science: An investigative journey through the world's religions* (Auckland: The Deepsight Trust, 1998). A fresh study of the rise of modern science written from the perspective of comparative religion.

2

Ways of seeing

There was once a man who thought he was dead and he went about telling people so. Understandably, his relatives engaged a psychiatrist to try to convince him that he was deluded. The psychiatrist eventually hit on what seemed a sure way of dispelling the man's delusion. He decided to begin by convincing his patient that dead men do not bleed. He therefore sent him off to the local library with a list of medical books to consult, took him to talk with eminent doctors and took him to visit some hospitals to see post-mortems performed. Eventually, the man admitted that he was utterly convinced that dead men do not bleed. At this the psychiatrist produced a knife and slashed the patient's arm, which bled profusely. The man stared at his bleeding wound, turned very pale and eventually stammered, 'Dead men *do* bleed!'

If people believe something very strongly, they will do all they can to force the evidence to the contrary to fit in with their beliefs, rather than change their minds.

Scientists are not supposed to be like that. The traditional, widely held view of how scientists arrive at conclusions is something like the following.

The scientist begins by collecting observational data in a purely objective way, free from all prejudices about the subject being studied, with no preferences concerning what theory might be correct and not hampered by any religious or philosophical ideas. In time, hopefully, some order or pattern will become apparent in the data. The scientist will try to summarize this pattern (preferably in a mathematical form) as a law. Then, by a process known as induction, the scientist will try to arrive at some wider generalizations and principles to connect together several laws. This produces a theory. In some cases more than one theory might emerge. The scientist will then try to deduce from the different theories some predictions which can be tested by observation. Hopefully, the predictions of only one theory will eventually stand up to testing.

Scientific teaching about the world

This account of the scientific method has some truth in it. Apart from anything else, it does draw attention to some of the characteristics of science. So far we have used the term 'science' without really defining it. In fact it is not easy to define. That does not mean that it is a meaningless or useless term. Try defining what you mean by 'love'. It is not easy, but that does not stop us saying, 'I love you,' or being able to tell the difference between a loving and an unloving action. While there is no simple, agreed definition of science, there are certain characteristics which are generally agreed to mark certain types of activity or pieces of work as 'scientific'.

Firstly, science is concerned with the natural world of

material things and events. Moreover, it looks for explanations of these things and events in terms of matter and energy alone. This separates science from philosophy and theology; science is concerned with the mechanism of the world but philosophy and religion are interested in such things as meanings, purposes and values.

Secondly, science is based on what actually happens in the natural world, which is studied by observation and experiment. It may be fun to dream up a bright idea and then theorize about its possible implications, but that is simply science fiction unless the idea can be shown to be rooted in events in the material world.

Thirdly, the links which scientists make between pieces of data, or between laws, have to be rational ones. Using mathematics to describe what they think is happening is one way of ensuring this.

Scientists aim to be objective in their work. In other words, they try not to let their own personal preferences or beliefs influence them. For this reason, only those observations and experiments which can be repeated by other people (under suitable conditions and with relevant training) are acceptable as scientific data.

A lot more could be said about the nature of science, but for our purposes it is enough to say that it is the attempt to carry out by observation and experiment a relatively objective study of the material world aiming at rational, materialistic explanations of what goes on in that world.

Facts and theories

Our description of how scientists work is a description of the ideal. In practice, no-one does, or could, work that way.

31

Scientists are always selective in the data or 'facts' which they collect. This may be because they can only spend limited time or money in searching for the data. Besides this, they will usually have a particular reason for making the observations or doing the experiment, often the desire to prove or disprove a theory. This means that, before they start looking, they already have an idea of the sort of data they want to find. The way someone has been trained, together with that person's past experience, will also affect the way he or she sees and collects data. This can be a good thing. A doctor can see significant things in an X-ray picture which a non-medical person would not. Of course, this training can mean that a person comes to the data with certain fixed expectations which blind her or him to some aspects of it. Similarly, if a scientist is committed to a particular theory, he or she can, quite unwittingly, overlook data or see it in a biased way, a bit like the 'dead' man in our story.

All in all, scientists are becoming much more aware that the line between facts and theories is a fuzzy one. Theories are attempts to make sense of facts, but what we see as facts, and how we assess them, is affected by the theories we already hold (or reject). As philosophers of science sometimes put it, all facts are to some extent 'theory-laden'.

Theories and reality

There is much debate today among philosophers of science about whether scientific theories tell us anything about the real world and, if they do, in what way. To a large extent this debate arises because of the loss of the Christian basis for science. Certainly the Christian believes that the scientist is studying a *real* world with a mind which is patterned on that of the world's creator and which can therefore understand the world as it really is. So the Christian will accept that what scientists tell us about the world does indeed correspond to reality.

However, the relationship between a theory and reality is not simple and straightforward. On the one hand, the fact that some theories last for centuries, successfully accounting for all the available data, might lead us to regard theories as simple descriptions of reality. On the other hand, since some theories come and go very quickly, we might be tempted to think of theories as not much more than figments of the imagination, soon dispelled by a dose of reality. The truth is somewhere in between these extremes.

There are two ways of thinking about scientific theories that are quite popular at the moment. One compares them to maps. In my map of London every symbol corresponds to some real feature of London. The red lines correspond to roads and the thickness of the lines to the width of the roads. The blue areas correspond to ponds, lakes and rivers. When I show someone the map, I do not claim that it *is* London, but I do claim that it corresponds to a real city and will enable them to find their way around it. Similarly, it is argued, scientific theories are not to be confused with reality itself but they do correspond to it, and help us to find our way around in it.

Another way of looking at theories is to regard them as mental 'models'. Most people, including most scientists, find it easier to think in pictures than in words or mathematical equations. For this reason many 'models' used by scientists are mental pictures. For example, one can think of a gas in terms of the 'billiard ball model'. This sees a gas as a lot of minuscule billiard balls in an enclosed box, always moving about, bounding off each other and the walls of the box. In fact, by applying Newton's laws of motion to this model it is possible to obtain a fairly good mathematical description of how gases actually behave. But no-one believes that gases really *are* made up of minuscule billiard balls. There is a lot of evidence to prove otherwise! The model is not a simple description of reality but key features of the model do correspond to features of the real world. In this way, the model helps us to understand and control the world. We only have refrigerators in our homes because the scientific model of how gases behave showed how they could be used as coolants.

This discussion of the nature of scientific theories has two important things to say to us as we consider how scientific knowledge and the Bible relate to one another. On the one hand, it tells us that we cannot simply brush aside scientific theories by saying, 'Oh, that's only a theory!' Good theories do relate to the realities of the material world. On the other hand, it warns us not to tie our understanding of the Bible too closely to any one theory, because theories are only representations of reality and will come and go as science advances.

This faces interpreters of the Bible with a dilemma. 'How far should I go in taking theory x into account, since theories come and go?' There is no simple answer to this but there are some useful guidelines.

Firstly, every theory has been produced to account for a set of data. Even if we do not take the theory into account, we will probably have to take note of the data. When a theory is discarded, the data on which it is based do not disappear but have to be explained in some other way. For example, the theory of evolution arose partly to account for the fossil data. If we reject the theory of evolution, whether for biblical or scientific reasons, we have to provide an alternative theory that explains the fossil evidence.

Secondly, whether we like it or not, we have to say something about those theories which are well known and widely held. People will not take us seriously in other areas unless we do. They will see us as irrelevant, avoiding the issues which interest them.

Thirdly, at any one time there are those theories which responsible scientists regard as well established and which provide a reliable basis for further scientific advance. We have got to take these seriously. We must see what their implications are, if any, for our interpretation of the Bible and for Christian thought. An example of this is the quantum theory and its implication that 'chance' or 'random' events play an important part in the fundamental processes of the universe. We will look at this later.

Testing theories

A theory links together laws, which in turn are derived from observational or experimental data. So theories stand at some distance from the data. What is a good theory, and how does a theory come to be regarded as well established?

There are a number of characteristics which scientists look for in a good theory. They are:

• *Consistency*. There should be no logical contradictions between the different parts or concepts which make up the theory.

• *Coherence*. It should be possible to make a variety of connections between the different concepts within the theory and with other theories.

• *Simplicity*. The number of assumptions involved should be small. Almost any theory can be made to work if enough arbitrary assumptions are allowed!

• *Comprehensiveness.* It should help us to see a unity underlying apparently diverse phenomena. If a theory can absorb the theory it replaces, that is a strong point in its favour. For example, the theory of relativity includes Newton's theory of gravity as a special case.

• *Fruitfulness.* Scientists are most interested in theories which suggest new ideas, concepts, laws and experiments rather than those which simply summarize existing ones.

• *Elegance.* This is hard to define. It often refers to the way in which the theory can be expressed mathematically.

However well a theory scores in terms of these six characteristics, scientists will want to test it experimentally. This is done by using the theory to make predictions which can be tested in some way. These, of course, should be predictions that rival theories do not make. For instance, Einstein's general theory of relativity predicted that massive bodies such as the sun should bend light. Newton's theory of gravity predicted a similar bending of light, but to a much smaller degree. It was the observation of the extent of the bending of light by the sun which convinced many physicists that Einstein's theory had to be taken seriously.

A theory may stand up to many such tests but it can never be said to have been absolutely proved. It is always possible that someone will think of yet one more test which will cause it to fail – as was the case with Newton's theory of gravity after more than 200 years. A theory can be disproved by its failure in just one test but it can never be proved conclusively. All the same, it seems reasonable to have more confidence in a theory the more tests it passes.

At this point it must be said that a theory is not always immediately abandoned simply because it fails a single experimental test. It may be that the failure can be overcome by a fairly minor modification of the theory. Even if this is not the case, a theory that has stood for quite a while and proved to be useful will not be readily abandoned until there is something better to put in its place. Scientists would rather work with a theory that they know is somewhat defective than have no theory at all. It is this reason, and not just stubbornness or obscurantism, that makes biologists cautious about throwing over the theory of evolution even though there are discrepancies and loose ends in it. At the moment, they are not convinced that there is anything better with which to replace it.

If it is true that theories are maps or models of reality, then we can assume that as better theories replace earlier ones, scientists are achieving better and better representations of, or approximations to, the reality of the material world.

It is sometimes claimed that theories of origins (of the universe, of life) are in a different class from other theories because they relate to unique, unrepeatable and, for us, unobservable events. However, it is not clear that this makes them all that different. Few theories, if any, relate to readily repeated and observed events in a simple, direct way. Theories of origins can be evaluated by the six criteria listed earlier in the same way as other theories. They, too, can be tested by their predictions.

The 'big bang' theory of the origin of the universe proposed that the universe began with a massive explosion of energy. As things cooled down, various atoms were formed. These then formed gas clouds, out of which galaxies and stars came into being. Among other things, this explained the apparent expansion of the universe which is observed today. In the 1960s this was opposed by the 'steady state' theory. This said that, as the universe expands, new matter appears in space to keep the density of matter in the universe more or less constant. The 'big bang' theory triumphed, partly because it predicts that radio astronomers should be able to observe background radiation left over from the initial 'big bang'. They have done this. The 'steady state' theory does not predict the existence of this radiation.

Scientific laws

So far we have said little about scientific laws or 'the laws of nature,' as they are often called. There is one misconception about them which needs to be cleared up.

Unfortunately, the word 'law' is used in science in a rather different way from its everyday use. In common speech, a law is a *prescription*, a statement about what you are supposed to do or not do. The speed-limit laws are an example. In science, a law is a *description*. It is a statement about a pattern that has been observed in the way things happen in the material world. It is like the statement of someone doing a road survey who says that 10% of the motorists were travelling faster than the speed limit. A scientific law does not say that this is the way things *have to happen*, but simply that this is the way things *have been seen to happen* under certain circumstances in the past. This is why scientific laws, like theories, are always open to revision in the light of new observations and fresh understanding of the world. It is also why the laws of nature cannot be said to rule out miracles; but that is another story.

Christian teaching about the world

We have looked so far at understanding the world in purely scientific terms. Some may wonder whether there is any other way of understanding it. That brings us back to chapter 1 and the different questions which science and religion ask about the world. Science asks, 'How has the universe come about?' and may answer in terms of the 'big bang' theory. Religion asks, 'Why is the universe here at all?' Christianity answers in terms of a creator God and his purposes. We will look more closely at this answer later in this book. In reality, the interests of science and religion are not quite as sharply differentiated as this how?/why? distinction suggests, as we shall see later.

The scientific understanding of the world is expressed in theories which are ultimately derived from data or 'facts' about the world. These theories can be evaluated and tested, as we have seen. What 'data' or 'facts' provide the Christian 'theory' – Christian teaching? And how can that teaching be evaluated and tested?

The primary data for Christian teaching is the Bible, along with our experience of life in the world interpreted in the light of the Bible's teaching. This is not the place to discuss why Christians believe the Bible to be the inspired Word of God and therefore reliable as the basis for their understanding of the world. For that you will need to go to other books. What we will discuss here is how Christian teaching can be evaluated and tested.

Doctrines as models

Philosophers of religion have pointed out that, just as scientific theories can be looked at as models, so can Christian doctrines.

Much Christian talk about God consists of mental pictures or models – God as father, mother, judge, rock and so on. God is not literally a parent or judge as we know them in human terms. God is obviously not an actual physical rock! These models pick out certain characteristics (source of existence, love, justice, reliability) and claim that they are true of the reality we call God. Talking of what Jesus has done for us as redemption or justification is also to use models, ones drawn from the experiences of the freeing of captives and acquittal in court.

Recognizing that Christian doctrines are like models of reality helps us to avoid equating them with the reality which they try to describe. Just as scientific theories are always open to revision or replacement in the light of new data, so Christian doctrines must be open to revision in the light of fresh understanding of the Bible.

The characteristics that are looked for in good theories also apply, with a little modification, to Christian doctrines: consistency, coherence, simplicity, comprehensiveness, fruitfulness and elegance.

At this point it might be objected that a doctrine like that of the Trinity violates the characteristic of consistency, since surely there is a logical contradiction involved in talking about one God existing as three persons. Part of the answer to this is to define carefully what theologians mean by 'person', but we will not stop to do that here. Besides this, we could say that it is not illogical when you recognize that the reality about which we are trying to speak is of a different, far more complex, order of being than we are. God is not limited to space, time and matter as we are. So we should not be surprised that talking about God stretches the capacity of our language and models. In fact, to make a reasonably adequate attempt to describe

40

God as he has revealed himself to us in the Bible, we have to use both the model of oneness and the model of three persons.

The use of such apparently incompatible models is known in science as well. The classic case is in the description of the behaviour of the electron. In some situations it is best described by the model of a particle, a minuscule billiard ball. In others it behaves like a wave, like a ripple in the water. The theory of the electron has to incorporate both models to do justice to all that is known about it. There is no logical contradiction involved because there are no situations when *both* models can be applied at the same time and give contradictory predictions. The doctrine of the Trinity has been constructed carefully by Christian theologians so that it does not lead to self-contradictory 'predictions' or statements about God and God's activity in the world.

Ultimately, scientific theories are tested by their 'fit' with the world. How well they fit is discovered by testing the predictions they make about the world. Christian doctrine is tested in much the same way. Does it make sense in my life as I live in obedience to it? Does it make more sense of the world than other religions or philosophies which clamour for attention? This does not make Christianity purely individualistic and subjective because I can, and should, take into account whether or not it makes sense of other people's experience too. This is like the need for the tests of scientific theories to be open to repetition by other people.

Another aspect of the objectivity of Christianity is its historical basis. A series of historical events lies at the heart of Christianity. Some of these are shared with Judaism, because both religions share the Hebrew Bible/Old Testament. However, the distinctively Christian event is the birth, life, death and resurrection of Jesus. Christians claim that this has to be taken into account in any attempt to explain the meaning and purpose of life in this world.

The role of faith

Faith plays a big part in both Christianity and science. Christianity is about having faith in Christ. This is often thought to highlight an irrational element in Christianity. Science, on the other hand, is supposed not to involve faith but to rest purely on what can be proved rationally.

There are two misconceptions here.

The first is that faith has no place in science. In fact, faith is fundamental to science. Scientists believe without absolute proof (that is, they have faith) that the world is ordered in a rational way and that this order is stable. Moreover, they believe without absolute proof (that is, they have faith) that the human mind is rational and can discover and understand that order correctly. It is not possible to do science without taking these basic steps of faith. We have seen that originally these beliefs were derived from Christian teaching. Without that basis they just hang in the air. It might be argued that they have been proved by the fact that they work. But do they work? Might not all scientists be suffering from a mass delusion like the 'dead man' at the start of this chapter? Some philosophers of science, having no time for the Christian basis of science, come close to suggesting as much.

Life as a Christian begins by putting one's faith in Christ as the saviour through whom we are brought back into a right relationship with our Creator. The second misconception is to think that this act of faith is irrational. It is certainly a step beyond what can be proved with no shadow of doubt. However, most Christians would claim that it is a *reasonable* step. There is plenty of evidence in the Bible and in the experience of Christians down the ages that Jesus is who he claimed to be, and that the commitment of one's life to him leads to the experience of God which is promised in the Bible. In other words, Christian faith is a reasoning and reasonable trust in Christ, based on a good deal of historical and experiential evidence, which is available to those who wish to investigate it.

Complementary views of reality

We will end this chapter by considering how the scientific and Christian view of the world relate to each other. The simple way of putting this is to say that they are complementary views of reality. We need both of them in order to complete our understanding of reality. We need answers to both the 'How?' and the 'Why?' questions. These answers are neither contradictory nor mutually exclusive. They complement one another. However, this does not mean that they can exist in complete isolation from each other. Sometimes the answers given to the 'How?' questions will have implications for the 'Why?' questions, and vice versa.

Physicists currently talk about fluctuations in a 'quantum vacuum' somehow snowballing and resulting in a 'big bang', leading to the universe as we know it. For the Christian this, if true, is a statement of how God chose to create the universe we know. Christian doctrine gives some reasons why he created it. We shall come to these in the second part of this book. However, the scientific answer gives a large role to 'chance', and the Christian answer says that there is a good purpose at work. The implications of these seemingly different claims need to be considered carefully if the two answers are to be regarded as complementary.

Scientists have discovered laws of nature. Some talk as if these somehow shut God out of the world and prevent him acting in it, if he exists at all. However, for Christians these are God's laws, and God is free to override them if he wishes. But there is more to it than that. The Bible teaches that God did not just create the world and then stand back to let it get along on its own. God is constantly sustaining it. Perhaps the right way to think of the laws of nature is to see them as God's normal way of acting in the world, keeping it in being. Sometimes God may choose, for good reasons, to act differently – we call this a miracle.

We could go on showing how the scientific and Christian ways of looking at the world can fit together. A picture that is sometimes used to help illustrate how they do this is that of the architect's plans for a building. The architect will draw up plans of the different levels – the ground floor, the first floor, and so on if there are others. There will be a front elevation, side elevations, a back elevation. Taken individually, these drawings may not seem to be related to each other but, to a person who knows what they are, they all fit together and make sense, giving an impression of the whole structure.

It is worth noting that in each of the different drawings there are indications of a fuller picture. The ground-floor plan will indicate that there is a staircase and a lift-shaft – indications of at least one more floor level. The same feature may look quite different in different drawings, such as a door marked on a floor-plan and then seen in an elevation. So, for example, Christians point out that there are features of the physical world which suggest that religious questions need to be asked in order to get a fuller picture of reality.

This illustration needs some modification. The Christian view of reality is not just one architect's drawing on a par with others. It is more like the artist's impression of the finished building, which helps us to fit the other drawings together properly and make better sense of them. It is the overarching view. That view is founded on the Bible, and we will now turn to the question of how we can make sure that we understand the Bible properly.

Further reading

R. H. Bube, *Putting It All Together: Seven patterns for relating science to Christian faith* (Lanham, MD: University Press of America, 1995). The 'seven patterns' of the title do not exhaust all the possibilities, but the discussion of them raises most of the important issues regarding relating science to the Christian faith.

M. A. Jeeves and R. J. Berry, *Science, Life and Christian Belief* (Leicester: Apollos, 1998). Chapters 1–4 cover what has been discussed in this chapter in more detail.

A. O'Hear, *An Introduction to the Philosophy of Science* (Oxford: OUP, 1990). This is a good general introduction to the subject that is reasonably accessible to the non-specialist.

D. Ratzsch, *Science and Its Limits: The natural sciences in Christian perspective* (Downers Grove, IL: IVP, and Leicester: Apollos, 2000). A readable, specifically Christian, discussion of developments in the philosophy of science since the 1960s.

3

Understanding the Bible

'The trouble with the Bible is that it can be used to prove anything!' The fact that people can make that complaint says more about the way the Bible has been used – or misused – than about the Bible itself. Just because the Bible has been regarded as the authoritative source for Christian belief, Christians have all too often gone to great lengths to try to prove that it supported *their* point of view. As a result, some have ignored and violated all the normal rules of interpretation which they would apply when reading any other piece of literature.

Some Christians have been taught that they do not need to interpret the Bible. Professor Scholer of Northern Baptist Seminary in Chicago tells of an occasion when he preached in a church in Canada. As he greeted people at the door after the service, one man said to him, 'I guess, Professor, it's all right for you to interpret the Bible, but I'll just do what it says!' That man did not realize that he *cannot* 'just do what the Bible says'. He does, or tries to do, what *he understands* it to say. Behind that understanding lies an interpretation of what he has read in the Bible.

Have you ever taken something that was not yours; been somewhere that you know as a Christian you should not have been; looked covetously at something that was not yours? 'Yes', is almost certainly your answer. So why have you still got two hands, two feet, two eyes? After all, Jesus said, 'If your hand/foot/eye causes you to sin, cut it off' (Mark 9:43–47). Why haven't you done what the Bible says?

'Hold on a moment,' you might say; 'you are being too literalistic. Jesus was using vivid picture language.' As it happens I think you are right, but, in saying that, you are interpreting the Bible. It is not a question of *whether or not* we interpret it, but whether or not we do it *consciously and properly*, following the basic rules of interpretation.

To speak of 'rules of interpretation' might make the Bible sound a difficult book, one that only scholars can safely read. That is not the case. The Bible's main message of salvation is clear and plain to all who read it wanting to find the truth. Besides which, we take most of the rules of interpretation for granted anyway, because we apply them every time we read a newspaper, novel or notice on the church noticeboard. However, the Bible itself warns us that not everything in it is easy to understand. Peter says of Paul's letters:

> His letters contain some things that are hard to understand, which ignorant and unstable people distort, as they do the other Scriptures, to their own destruction (2 Peter 3:16).

The Bible refers also to the need for effort and study if

47

we are to learn how to handle it properly. Paul says to Timothy:

> Do your best to present yourself to God as one approved, a workman who does not need to be ashamed and who correctly handles the word of truth (2 Timothy 2:15).

So then, if we really do want to do what the Bible says, we will take seriously the task of learning how to interpret it.

An inspired Bible

Christians believe that the Bible is inspired by God. This is what the Bible claims for itself in various places (e.g. 2 Samuel 23:2; Jeremiah 1:9; 2 Timothy 3:16). It is not a claim that can be proved by any 'knock-down' argument. Christians find strong support for it in their experience that the Bible speaks to them in a way that no other book does, and in a way that they can only express by saying that God speaks through the Bible.

Some people think that to say that the Bible is 'inspired by God' means that God dictated the Bible to its authors, who were a bit like shorthand secretaries. But just a brief look at the contents of the Bible rules out this idea as too simplistic. There is clear evidence of very deep human involvement in the production of the Bible.

It seems that the writers of the historical books – books which tell the history of Israel – worked in the same way as other historians. They searched out sources, collated the information they gained, summarized some parts, quoted others in full, and so on. This is what seems to be implied by the frequent references to such sources (e.g. 1 Kings

11:41; 2 Chronicles 12:15). Luke tells us that he worked in a similar way when he wrote his Gospel (Luke 1:1–3). In the books of the prophets, the Gospels and the New Testament letters, the personalities of the writers are deeply woven into their writing. Each has his own writing style and his own favourite words and phrases (e.g. Matthew used the rabbinic phrase 'the kingdom of heaven', which avoids using the word 'God'; Luke uses 'the kingdom of God'). The writers of the Bible used ordinary human languages. The Greek of the New Testament is the Greek that was used in the homes and market places of the eastern Mediterranean world of that time. The books of the Bible did not drop from heaven. They were the result of much human thought, effort and literary activity on the part of the writers.

To say that the Bible is inspired by God is to say that all this thought, effort and activity was guided by God. This is not to say that God in some way violated the normal thought processes or personalities of the writers. Nor does it mean that the Bible must contain errors put there by the human authors. God, knowing each person's mind and personality inside out, could choose as writers those whom he knew would be able to understand what he wanted to convey and could pass it on without it becoming distorted.

In our modern communications systems, as every telephone-user knows, messages can be distorted by 'noise' in the system. If it is vital to avoid such distortion, experts can analyse the characteristics of the 'noise' and add to the message a signal which neutralizes the effects of the noise. The message then gets through undistorted. Surely God is capable of doing the same kind of thing when communicating with human beings!

The Bible, then, is a book that is both truly divine and

truly human. It is its humanness that has to be taken into account in the task of interpretation; being written by real people it is rooted in particular historical and cultural situations, and is expressed in languages and thought-forms that are not our own.

Interpreting the Bible

Where do we start? For most of us the starting-point is an English translation of the Bible. This is not a trivial point.

The Bible was originally written in Greek and Hebrew, with a few chapters in Aramaic. If we read it in English, therefore, we are dependent to some extent on the translators' interpretation of the original. This is because any translation translates not just words but meaning. A word-for-word translation often makes little sense because it ignores the peculiarities in grammar and idiom of the two languages concerned. A word-for-word translation of the beginning of Leviticus 26:26 is: 'When I break for you a staff of bread.' That is good idiomatic Hebrew but does not make much sense as an English sentence! What the original means is: 'When I cut off your supply of bread.' A good translator cannot avoid doing some interpretation but will try to keep it to a minimum. A translation, such as the *New International Version* or the *Revised Standard Version*, differs from a paraphrase, such as *The Living Bible* or *The New Testament in Modern English* by J. B. Phillips. Paraphrases are freer translations which contain a high degree of the translator's own interpretation. They can be refreshing reading but should never be used as a basis for serious Bible study.

When trying to understand a Bible passage, there are five rules of interpretation to follow.

1. *Compare translations*

Compare the passage you are studying with the same passage in at least two other good modern translations. This way you will probably be able to spot the places where the translators' interpretation of the original has had a substantial effect on the translation. You can then take this into account in your study of the passage.

2. *Use normal rules of language and literature*

Interpret what you read in terms of the normal rules of language and literature. The fact that the Bible is God's Word does not exempt it from these rules and enable you to make it mean whatever you want! On the contrary, God chose to express the message in the particular grammatical and literary forms that are used, in order to fix its meaning in this way.

There are many different ways of using language. It is important to recognize when language is to be taken literally, and when it is to be taken figuratively. We are all used to making a distinction between poetry and prose and readily allow for 'poetic licence'. In poetry we expect to find words used in ways which, if taken literally, are nonsensical. What the writer is after is not the literal meaning but the images conveyed, the emotions aroused. To say, as the psalmist does a number of times, 'God is my rock, my fortress', is literal nonsense, but the meaning is obvious to anyone with a grain of imagination.

It is not only in poetry that we use language in a non-literal sense. If I ask my wife how the day's teaching has gone and she says, 'I spent most of the afternoon banging my head against a brick wall,' I do not start looking for the bruises! If her words are taken literally, she has told me a lie. However, she has used language in a non-literal way to make a true statement about her experience in the classroom. This kind of 'figure of speech', as it is called, is in fact quite common in prose. We talk of a child being 'as bright as a button', of a friend as 'a tower of strength', someone else as 'a pillar of the church' and so on. These figures of speech are usually quite obvious to us in our own native language but are not always so easily spotted in a foreign language which may have its own, rather different set of images derived from its own cultural setting. This is a point to which we will return when studying Genesis 1 – 11.

Another aspect of this rule which we will need to consider when we come to look in detail at Genesis 1 – 11 is the importance of understanding and taking into account the type of literature which we are reading. The Bible is not a book but a collection of books. They are of many types: books of history, poetry, proverbs, prophecy, letters. Some books contain more than one type of literature. We can misunderstand a passage if we are not clear about the type of literature to which it belongs.

'What is a proverb?' I asked. 'A wise saying', 'A piece of good advice', were two of the answers I got. If that is so, what should we make of Proverbs 21:14? That verse reads:

> A gift given in secret soothes anger,
>> and a bribe concealed in the cloak pacifies
>> great wrath.

Does this mean that we should give bribes? It does if proverbs are good advice – but they are not. Hebrew proverbs, at least, are *realistic observations* on life expressed in an easy-to-remember form. They do not necessarily express a moral judgment. Proverbs 21:14 simply makes the observation that bribes sometimes succeed. This is what makes it so tempting to use them. However, Proverbs 17:23 does pass a moral judgment on the practice:

> A wicked man accepts a bribe in secret
> to pervert the course of justice.

This raises another important point. It is dangerous to take a small part of a passage or book and interpret it in isolation from the rest. The book of Proverbs' teaching on bribes cannot be decided on the basis of 21:14 alone. We must consider all the proverbs about bribes which are contained in the book.

3. Harmonize rather than oppose

If we believe that the Bible is the inspired Word of God, we would not expect it to contradict itself, since we would not expect God, who is faithful and true, to say one thing at one time and then contradict himself at some other time. When we come across apparent contradictions (like Proverbs 17:23 and 21:14), we will expect that further thought and study will show how the two passages should be harmonized. However, we must not twist passages in order to force a harmony. Sometimes we just have to admit that we do not yet have an answer to the apparent contradiction. It may be that in time some fresh evidence or new insight will resolve the contradiction.

4. Look for the original meaning

Establish what the passage would have meant to the original writer and his readers. To do this we have to learn all we can about the language, history and culture of the time. There are two aspects of this that will be of particular importance to our study of Genesis 1 – 11.

Can we believe Genesis today?

The form of literature

The first aspect concerns the different forms of literature in the Old Testament. When discussing proverbs earlier I was careful to give the definition of a Hebrew proverb. In other languages and cultures, proverbs might have a different character. The Hebrew proverbs in the Old Testament are similar in both form and content to Egyptian and Mesopotamian proverbs. We therefore have quite a large amount of proverbial material from the Ancient Near East, from which we can get a good idea of the nature and purpose of proverbs in those cultures. This gives a good basis for interpreting Old Testament proverbs correctly.

We need to treat the historical material in the Old Testament in the same sort of way. A good deal of similar material exists from Ancient Egypt and Mesopotamia, from which we can discover the characteristics of history-writing at that time. Old Testament historical passages must be understood in the light of *these* characteristics, not in the light of how history is written in the twenty-first century AD.

Similarly, when we look at Genesis 1 – 3 we will need to see whether other Ancient Near Eastern creation stories throw any light on the way in which these chapters should be understood.

Scientific and biblical language

The second aspect concerns the different characteristics of scientific and biblical language. One mark of modern science is that it has developed its own kind of language. Scientists use words carefully – or should do. Terms are carefully defined and used as precisely as possible. In chapter 4 we will see that the way in which the words 'chance' and 'random' are defined in science is rather different from, and more precise than, their use in ordinary speech.

The Bible is not written in scientific language. On the whole, it is written in the popular language of the common people of the time. There are exceptions to this in some of the terms used for the rituals of the temple in the Old Testament, and in the more theological use of some words in the letters of Paul in particular (even though these were written to ordinary people). The important point to note is that in the areas of most interest to science – where the Bible speaks about the natural world – the Bible uses popular language.

This language has three particular characteristics:

• *It is not very precise.* There have been attempts to show that Genesis 1 teaches that species are permanently fixed and cannot evolve. This is because of the repeated statement that the plants and animals produced offspring 'according to their kind'. The Hebrew word 'kind' (*mîn*) is taken to mean the same as the scientific term 'species'. This just does not stand up to examination. Looking up a concordance to study the uses of the word *mîn* in the Old Testament makes it clear that its use is far too imprecise to equate it with any of the modern biological terms such as 'species', 'genera' or whatever. It is best translated by an imprecise English word such as 'kind'!

• *It is the language of appearance*, describing things as they appear to be to the ordinary observer. The Bible speaks of the sun 'rising' and 'setting', just as most people do today. (We do not, for instance, say, 'Look, because of the rotation of the earth the sun is disappearing below our line of sight.') The statement about animals reproducing 'according to their kind' probably expresses nothing more than the fact we all observe that dogs have puppies, not kittens. It should not be taken to rule out the possibility that major changes might occur over many generations.

• *It is full of cultural idioms.* Some of these idioms reflect what might be called popular 'science', if you are prepared to stretch the meaning of 'science'. For example, there are frequent references in the Old Testament to people thinking, deciding, meditating on things 'in their heart'. There is no doubt that the Hebrew word here (*lēb*) does refer to the physical organ in the chest (e.g. 2 Kings 9:24). There is no known separate Hebrew word for 'mind'. It may be that the Hebrews connected the heart with thought processes because sometimes there is a correlation between the rate of our heartbeat and what we are thinking. This is no different in principle from the way in which we link the heart with the emotions, because strong emotions affect our heartbeat. Scientifically, we are no more correct than the Hebrews. If emotions are to be connected with any bodily organ it ought to be with the endocrine glands. However, the Hebrews knew what they meant when they said, 'I pondered in my heart what to do,' just as we know what we mean when we say, 'I love you with all my heart.' There is no problem, unless someone insists that everything that the Bible says must be taken as scientifically accurate, totally ignoring the culturally bound, idiomatic use of language.

5. Look for the original intention

Finally, we come to our fifth rule of interpretation. This is that we must be guided in our interpretation by the author's original intention. What was he intending to talk about? To come back to our previous example, if it were clear that any of the Old Testament references to people thinking or planning in their hearts was *intended* to teach us about human physiology or psychology, then we would have a clash between the Bible and modern science. However, this was not the intention of those authors. Similarly, we will have to see whether there is any evidence to help us decide what the author of Genesis 1 – 3 intended to teach his readers. How far, if at all, was he concerned with explaining *how* God created the earth and living things? Was he perhaps only really concerned with telling us *why* God did it and what that means for the way we are to live our lives on earth? These are going to be crucial questions in the next chapter.

Truth and error

If the Bible is the inspired Word of God in the way that we suggested at the beginning of this chapter, then we would expect it to be free from error. God knows everything, so does not suffer, as we do, from ignorance. He is perfectly wise, so does not make mistakes. He is the truth, so will not lead us off course in our search for truth. For these kinds of reasons, orthodox Christians have spoken of the Bible being 'infallible', 'inerrant' or 'trustworthy'.

At this point it is important to remember what we have discussed above about interpreting the Bible. Otherwise we will misunderstand the meaning of the 'inerrancy' of the Bible. If we misinterpret the Bible, it is not the Bible that is in error, we are. Listen to this imaginary sixteenth-century conversation between an astronomer (A) and a biblical scholar (BS):

A: I have proved that the Bible is wrong!
BS: Where? In what way?
A: In your commentary on Genesis 1:16, don't you stress that the Hebrew says, 'And God

> made *the* two great lights', and that this means
> that the sun and the moon are the two biggest
> heavenly bodies?
>
> BS: Yes, that's true.
>
> A: Well, using the newly invented telescope, I
> have proved that the planet Saturn is much
> bigger than the moon. Therefore the Bible is
> wrong!
>
> BS: It can't be! Your measurements and calcu-
> lations must be wrong!
>
> A: They're not! Two other astronomers have
> checked them. If you don't believe me, come
> and see for yourself.
>
> BS: No fear! The telescope is clearly an invention
> of the devil intended to lead people like you
> astray! I'm not going to look through it!

That conversation is not purely imaginary. This issue was
being debated in the sixteenth century, and John Calvin
refers to it in his commentary on Genesis. He blames
some scholars for making the Bible look silly by
misinterpreting it and then insisting on the truth of their
interpretation against all the evidence of the astronomers.
In dealing with this issue, Calvin appeals to two of the
rules of interpretation we have discussed above.

The language of appearance

Firstly, using the rule of finding the original meaning,
Calvin argues that the language used in Genesis 1, as
everywhere else when the Bible speaks about natural
phenomena, is the common 'language of appearance'. The
sun and the moon *appear* to be the largest and brightest of
the heavenly bodies. All readers of Genesis down the ages

have had no difficulty in understanding what is meant by 'the two great lights'. We know now that Jupiter is the biggest planet. If the language of Genesis 1:16 was meant to be scientifically precise, and so refer to the sun and to Jupiter (which seems impossible anyway, since how can Jupiter be said to 'rule the night' as the sun does the day?), then all readers down the ages (and many today) would have been misled, since they would be bound to think that the reference is to the sun and the moon.

Purpose

Secondly, in line with understanding the original intention, Calvin insists that the purpose of Genesis 1, and indeed of the Bible, is not to teach astronomy but to lead us to see our need for salvation and to find it through faith in Christ. To think that astronomical information can be gleaned from Genesis 1 is to misunderstand the author's intention and so to misinterpret the passage.

Calvin's approach to this kind of issue is summed up by a comment he makes in his commentary on Psalm 136:

> The Holy Spirit had no intention to teach astronomy; and in proposing instruction meant to be common to the simplest and most uneducated person, he made use by Moses and other prophets of the popular language that none might shelter himself under the pretext of obscurity.

Of course, Calvin was a man of his time and quite capable of making mistakes. For example, he assumed that for the moon to be a 'light' it must be a hot, burning body. After all, the lights that Calvin knew did all involve burning something (wood, oil, wax, etc). We know now that the moon is only a reflector of sunlight. If the Holy Spirit had been interested in scientific instruction, surely Genesis 1:16 should have read, 'And God made a great light and a great reflector/mirror'!

It will be helpful at this point to sum up what we can learn from this example:

• Christians who believe that the Bible is free from error cannot claim that the same applies to their interpretations of the Bible.

• The claim that the Bible is free from error *must* include a proper understanding of the types of literature and language used in the Bible, and of the original intention of the authors.

• If, as Christians, we are not scrupulously careful in our interpretation of the Bible and humble in the presentation of what we think it means, we will bring the Bible into disrepute by creating unreal errors in it. If we insist, as some medieval scholars did, that Genesis 1:16 must be taken literalistically (ignoring the kind of language used) as a source of astronomical information (ignoring the true purpose of the passage), then we have no defence when the astronomers turn round and say that they have proved that it contains two scientific errors about the size and nature of the moon.

Science and the Bible

We are now in a position to answer the question, 'How should we relate the findings of science to what we read in the Bible?'

First of all, what we have just said about interpreting the Bible warns us that we must be very careful in this area. We can only claim that a Bible passage provides information of a scientific kind when we are sure that this is warranted by the nature of the language in the passage, the type of literature to which it belongs, and the author's intention.

Secondly, if modern scientific findings seem to clash with the Bible, as we understand it, we must be prepared to re-examine our interpretation of the Bible. The scientists may be wrong and, if we have the expertise, we have the right to question and investigate the soundness of their claims. However, *we* may be wrong.

Just because the language of appearance is often the language of common sense, it is not always easy to recognize it except with hindsight. It seems obvious to us now that the biblical scholars who insisted that the Bible teaches that the earth is stationary, and that the sun moves round it, were reading the Bible in a wrongly literalistic way. But it was not so obvious to them, partly because it seems common sense to see things that way: you know when you are on a moving cart; surely it would be obvious if we were on a moving earth! Three hundred years or more of modern science have taught us that common sense is not always a good guide to understanding the wonders of God's creation. Indeed, a good deal of what science has shown about the creation is counter-intuitive, not to say mind-bending. But this is what we might expect, given the limitations of our finite minds compared with the mind of the Creator.

Science can in fact help us to avoid mishandling the Bible by helping us to recognize where we might be mis-interpreting it. Some people are afraid that to talk like this is to subordinate the Bible to science. It is not. Perhaps an example from another area of study will help here.

A century or so ago there were a number of Greek words in the New Testament whose meaning was obscure.

Can we believe Genesis today?

This was because they occur only rarely in the New Testament, in difficult contexts, and were not known in other Greek literature. Then, at the end of the nineteenth century, a lot of Greek documents were discovered, preserved in the hot, dry sand of Egypt. Many of those obscure Greek words were found in them, in sentences where their meaning was clear. In some cases the meanings that had been proposed by New Testament scholars were confirmed, in others they were shown to be incorrect. No-one would complain that scholars were subordinating the Bible to language study by correcting their previous understanding of these words and so of the passages in which they occur. It was, rather, a case of subordinating their interpretation to the newly discovered truth. This is what we have to do with newly discovered scientific truth – once that truth has been well established. The situation with regard to scientific truth will often not be as clear-cut as in the example I have given, but that is no excuse for ignoring the principle that responsible interpretation of the Bible must take into account the best available knowledge we have from all areas of study.

This too is a principle which John Calvin recognized. In his *Institutes of the Christian Religion*, Book 2, he says,

> If we hold the Spirit of God to be the only source of truth, we will neither reject nor despise the truth, wherever it may reveal itself, lest we offend the Spirit of God (2.2.15).

The Bible is true, but it does not contain all the truth about everything. God has given us minds and abilities to search for truth outside of the Bible. When we find it, it too is God's truth. We are then right to use it to help us understand the Bible more clearly – whether it be the results of language study, archaeology, history or even science. The fact is that we never can, or do, interpret the Bible in isolation. We always bring to the task what knowledge we have. We therefore have the responsibility to bring to it the best available knowledge.

The authority of the Bible

If the Bible is the inspired, inerrant Word of God, then we ought to accept it as authoritative. We should listen to it, humbly accept what it says and then obey it. Does what has just been written, about using truth from other sources to help us understand the Bible properly, in any way lessen its authority? Not at all. The authority of the Bible is nothing other than the authority of God the Holy Spirit who inspired its writers. As we have seen, the same Holy Spirit is the source of all truth, which therefore bears his authority. To use that truth in interpreting the Bible is another way of submitting to the authority of the ultimate author of the Bible. While saying this, we need to recognize that the truth presented by human scholars in any field will have limitations because of the finiteness of our minds, and also because our fallenness means that sometimes we might distort the truth for a variety of reasons. But then the same is true of our interpretation of the Bible. One of the values of bringing our wider knowledge to the task of understanding the Bible is that, in the resulting 'dialogue', the wider knowledge can sometimes help us see where our interpretation of the Bible may be going astray and, conversely, our understanding of the knowledge gained from elsewhere may be modified in the light of Scripture.

When Christians disagree

Finally, before we turn to our study of Genesis 1 – 11, we need to consider briefly the question of what we should do when we find that equally sincere and Bible-believing Christians differ from one another and from oneself in their understanding of what the Bible teaches. This, of course, is the case with Genesis 1 – 11.

I would suggest that, with God's help, we need to cultivate the following set of attitudes.

1. *Humility.* We need the humility to recognize that there may be a difference between what the Bible says and what we think it says. We may have misunderstood it, and should be ready to re-examine, and perhaps change, our interpretation.

2. *Self-awareness.* All kinds of factors predispose us to accept some interpretations while resisting others – our personality, background, experience, friends. Someone who works as a scientist may find it hard to question what the great majority of scientists simply accept as 'obviously' true. Most of us find it hard to question the inter-pretations of disputed passages of the Bible that are widely accepted among our Christian friends or in our church tradition. We need to ask God to search us and show us where we are being influenced by these kinds of factors and so are not being truly open to his word in the Bible.

3. *Integrity.* Some people are unwilling ever to read or consider anything with which they think they might disagree, no doubt afraid that it might lead them to change their minds! This is an unhealthy and dishonest attitude. It is right for a baby to be protected for a while as it gains strength before it is exposed to the world at large. Christians, however, should not remain perpetual babies (see Hebrews 5:11–14). We lack maturity and integrity if

we hold strongly to a view without having given serious consideration to alternatives. In any case, we claim to be following a God who is the truth, so we have nothing to fear in examining all sides of an issue. Quite the reverse. Our desire, surely, is to discover the truth – God's truth – and not just to be proved right!

4. *A sense of proportion.* Does it really matter if Christians disagree? Yes, but it does not always matter to the same extent. As Christians we should be seeking to be one in Christ and so to agree with one another. However, the fact is that as long as we live in this world, limited by our finite minds and still not fully free from sin, we are going to disagree. But not all disagreements are of equal importance. All Christian doctrines are interrelated to some extent. Nevertheless, some are more central to the Christian faith than others. Clearly, the message of salvation by grace through faith in Christ is of central importance. Disagreements over that are very serious because they go to the heart of what it means to be a Christian. Disagreements over how God created the world, and whether or not the Bible tells us this, would seem to belong to a different category, even though they do have some implications for our understanding of other doctrines. In some circles, however, acceptance of particular views about this becomes almost a test of salvation: 'You are not really a Christian unless you have been saved by grace through faith in Christ *and* believe that ...' I believe that this comes dangerously near to adding something to the gospel other than faith in Christ.

5. *Love.* Many disagreements can be lived with and then perhaps eventually settled, if those who disagree treat one another with love. We are called to love one another because Christ loved us enough to die for us, not because we agree with one another! That should enable us to pray,

discuss and live amicably with those with whom we disagree, while seeking to discover the truth together.

Further reading

G. D. Fee and D. Stuart, *How to Read the Bible for All its Worth* (London: SU, 1982). An excellent, fairly detailed guide to the task of biblical interpretation.

R. Forster and P. Marston, *Reason, Science and Faith* (Crowborough: Monarch, 1999). Chapter 6 provides an interesting survey of the different interpretations of Genesis 1 – 3 down through history; chapter 7 discusses its interpretation today.

G. Jones, *Coping with Controversy*, rev. ed. (Carlisle: Solway, 1996). A helpful book about how Christians can deal effectively with differences and controversy.

S. Motyer, *Unlock the Bible* (London: SU, 1990). A good, readable, introduction to interpreting the Bible.

4

Beginnings: a literal approach

Since the third century AD Christians have differed over whether or not Genesis 1 should be interpreted literally. Around AD 400 St Augustine of Hippo, one of the leading early theologians, argued in his commentaries on Genesis, his *Confessions* and in other writings, for a non-literal reading of the chapter. His reasons were theological, literary and philosophical, and obviously nothing to do with the theory of evolution!

It would require a very long book to describe and discuss all the various interpretations that have been offered for Genesis 1, not to mention the rest of chapters 1 – 11. We will therefore be simplifying and summarizing, with all the attendant risks of leaving out some ideas and arguments that others might consider important. The 'Further reading' suggestions at the end of this and the following chapters give a guide to books that present various positions in more detail. Most of the different positions can be grouped into one of the three types of approach: (1) literal; (2) concordist; and (3) literary-cultural. Within each group there are differences of approach. In this chapter we will consider only one type of literal approach. On the basis of my own experience of talking about these issues to both churches and Christian student groups, and also of surveying the books on sale in Christian bookshops, it seems a widely popular view among evangelical Christians.

A literal approach to Genesis 1:1 – 2:3

One of the ways of reading Genesis 1:1 – 2:3 (this is one of many examples of a biblical chapter division being put in an unfortunate place) is to take it literally, as a simple historical account of how God created the world. The attraction of this approach is that it seems so simple and obvious. It is the way most Christians have understood the chapter. Of course this is not conclusive. Christians traditionally took the references to the earth standing still to mean that it does not move and that the sun moves round it, until the findings of science showed that that interpretation had to be rethought. Besides which, as we have already noted, since the early Christian centuries, some have questioned the literal reading of this passage. Since serious study of geology and the fossils began in the eighteenth century, more and more Christians have questioned this approach.

Although the literal approach to Genesis 1:1 – 2:3 is simple in one way, it is far from simple in another. A vast body of literature has grown up to support it in the face of the findings of science over the last 200 years. There are three issues that have had most attention from those holding to the literal approach: the age of the earth, the fossils and the theory of evolution.

Debate about the age of the earth and the fossils predates the theory of evolution. In fact, before Darwin's *On the Origin of Species* was published in 1859, most Christian scholars, including those who held firmly to the view that the Bible is divinely inspired and therefore fully trustworthy, accepted that the earth was millions of years old, and they sought to understand the opening chapters of the Bible in the light of that. The modern version of the view that the earth is only thousands of years old, not millions, seems to have originated in the 1920s with the Seventh Day Adventist writer and teacher G. M. Price, who developed the ideas of the founder of Seventh Day Adventism, Ellen G. White. It gained popularity in evangelical circles following the publication of *The Genesis Flood* by J. Whitcomb and H. Morris (Grand Rapids, MI: Baker, 1961). Today this view is often referred to as the 'creation science' view. However, this is a bit misleading. Those who adopt both of the other approaches that we will discuss consider themselves 'creationists', and some would want to insist that their approach is also scientific. A more accurate description of this kind of literal approach is to say that it is the 'young earth, flood geology' view.

The age of the earth

The reason that it is a 'young earth' view is that a simple, literal, reading of Genesis 1:1 – 2:3 cannot be divorced from a similar reading of the rest of Genesis, including the genealogies. Most people are aware of Archbishop Ussher's calculations based on these, which date the flood to 2349 BC and the creation of Adam to 4004 BC. 'Young earth' advocates do not take these dates at face value. It would be difficult to do so, since there are plenty of written historical records from Egypt and Mesopotamia which come from before 2000 BC and make it clear that the flood could not have happened in 2349 BC. (The events recorded in these records can be dated with considerable accuracy, because the records include references to eclipses and other astronomical events that can now be dated to the minute by computer calculations based on the laws of planetary motion.) So, they usually argue that the genealogies are selective and incomplete (as, for example, the genealogy of Jesus in Matthew 1 is seen to be, when compared with Old Testament genealogies). As a result those who hold the 'young earth' view are usually happy to say that the earth was created about 10,000 years ago.

How then does this view deal with the scientific indications that the earth is about 4,500 million years old?

The earth simply 'appears' to be old

One way is to suggest that God created the world with 'an appearance of age'. This idea goes back to a book entitled *Omphalos*, written by P. Gosse in 1857. Gosse argued that, when God created Adam, he presumably created him with a navel (*omphalos* is the Greek for 'navel') so that he looked just like someone born as a baby. Moreover, presumably the trees in Eden had growth rings, just as trees that have grown naturally since have rings by which their age can be measured. In other words, a modern scientist transported back to Eden a few minutes after its creation would think that it had existed for decades or centuries. The same kind of argument can be applied to the geological strata, the fossils and all other indications of the age of the earth. There is no biblical evidence to help here, either for or against the theory.

If applied consistently, this argument means that we

must accept the findings of the scientists as accurate. They are measuring the age of the earth as God made it appear to be. To look for evidences of a different (younger) age would be to imply that God has been either inconsistent or incompetent in his creative work. The only way we can know the true age of the earth is from a literalistic reading of the Bible.

There are two difficulties with the view that the earth simply appears to be old. The first is that it means God's revelation in the Bible is to be taken at face value, though we are not to take his revelation in creation at face value. Secondly, and more seriously, it seems to make God guilty of deceiving even well-meaning investigators of his creation.

Some 'young earth' advocates appeal to the 'appearance of age' argument, yet also argue that there is evidence that the earth is only a few thousand years old. They do not seem to realize that the two forms of argument are incompatible. As we pointed out earlier, if the earth was created to look old, there should be no evidence that it is young.

Change of strength in magnetic field
A typical and popular example of the 'scientific' arguments for a young earth is the one that is based on changes in the strength of the earth's magnetic field. It is typical both in the form of the argument used, and in the weaknesses in it. It is, therefore, a good example to examine in some detail.

In 1973 Dr Thomas Barnes pointed out that the strength of the earth's magnetic field had decreased gradually over the previous 150 years. He plotted the values on a graph and then fitted what is called an 'exponential curve' (one whose value doubles at a fixed interval – every 1,400 years in the case of Barnes's curve) to the data. Then he extrapolated this backwards in time, assuming that the magnetic field strength had decreased steadily at this exponential rate throughout the earth's history. He concluded that the strength would have been absurdly high 20,000 years ago. Hence, the earth cannot be a great deal older than 10,000 years.

This conclusion, however, is not as obvious as it might at first appear to be, because there are a number of weaknesses in the argument.

Firstly, no scientist would normally extrapolate data by more than a factor of two or three. In other words, 150 years' worth of data would not normally be extrapolated back more than 500 years. This is because the slightest error in fitting the curve to the data gets magnified rapidly the further the data is extrapolated. Figure 1 (see opposite) shows the shape of the curve that Barnes used, and just how small is the portion of it that covers the period for which data is available.

Secondly, Barnes's data are quite scattered and by no means fit his curve perfectly. In that situation, an experienced scientist would not try to fit anything other than a straight line to the data. If this is done, the value of the magnetic field that Barnes regards as absurdly high is only reached after about 100 million years. Figure 2 shows the data with a 'best fit' straight line (see p. 74). Over this period, and at the scale of the diagram, there is no significant difference between Barnes's curve and the straight line. They begin to diverge significantly after about 300 years into the past (c. AD 1650), and the divergence then increases rapidly.

Thirdly, any extrapolation depends on a steady change in the value being measured. There is a lot of evidence that the rate of change of the earth's magnetic field has not

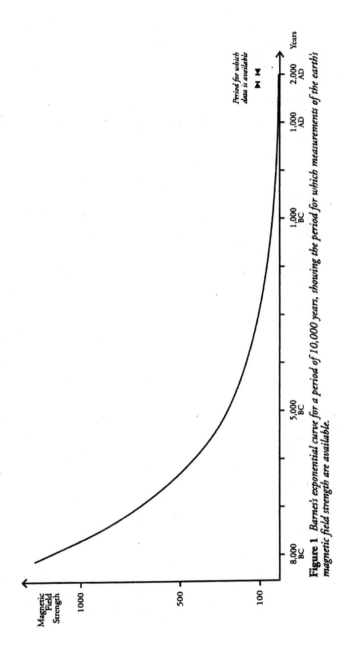

Figure 1 *Barnes's exponential curve for a period of 10,000 years, showing the period for which measurements of the earth's magnetic field strength are available.*

73

been steady. For one thing, the variation in the earth's magnetic field is not the same from place to place. Over a one-hundred-year period in Cape Town it decreased by 30%. This would suggest that the earth is only a few hundred years old! Moreover, geologists think that there is very good evidence from magnetic rocks that the strength of the earth's magnetism has oscillated up and down, and periodically reversed direction, rather than decreased steadily. The study of fired pottery provides evidence of the strength of the earth's magnetic field over the past few thousand years. This is because, when certain types of magnetic material are heated to a high temperature and then cooled, they are magnetized to the strength of the earth's magnetic field and this strength is 'locked in' when

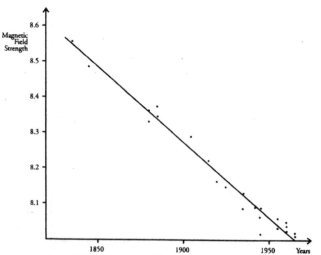

Figure 2 *The measurements of the strength of the dipole component of the earth's magnetic movement for 1835–1965, which were used by Barnes.*

they cool down. These studies show that the strength of the earth's magnetic field last peaked just over 2,000 years ago. Before then, it was increasing, and since then it has decreased.

Fourthly, Barnes's view, that the strength he calculates for the earth's magnetic field 20,000 years ago is absurdly high, depends on his theory of how the earth's magnetism is produced (the 'dissipating electric currents' theory). At present, geophysicists favour a different theory (the 'self-sustaining dynamo' theory) of its origin. According to this the value calculated by Barnes is not absurdly high. However, it must be said that the question of how the earth's magnetism is produced is still far from settled.

These weaknesses in the argument have been pointed out quite often. It is unfortunate that some books written in the mid-nineteen-nineties by 'young earth' advocates still refer to Barnes's argument as if it were quite conclusive, rarely mentioning the problems with it. One such book makes very selective use of the pottery data. It only quotes the evidence of the decreasing field strength since about 2,000 years ago, and ignores the evidence that before this the field strength was increasing (C. Mitchell, *The Case for Creationism*). This is not good science, and only brings creationism into disrepute, and the Bible with it.

R. Humphreys accepts the reality of the changes in the direction of the earth's magnetic moment but argues that there has been a continuous decay in the *energy* of the earth's magnetic field (see Appendix B in A. McIntosh, *Genesis for Today*). This argument, like Barnes's, depends on a particular model of how the magnetic field is produced, which is different from the currently widely accepted one.

On examination, many of the arguments for a young

earth seem to depend on questionable extrapolations of data or to rest on data whose significance is disputed – or both. This does not necessarily mean that they are wrong, but they do need to be treated with greater care and to be subjected to more critical examination than is usually the case. Also, the selective use of data quoted above is not an isolated example.

The evidence of radioactive dating

There are a number of different kinds of evidence put forward in favour of a great age for the earth; for example, the apparent expansion of the universe, the age of the oldest star clusters in our galaxy, the radioactive dating of rocks. These are all quite independent methods but all point to an age of 12,000–15,000 million years for the universe, and about 4,500 million years for the earth. Those who believe in a young earth concentrate their attack on the reliability of radioactive dating of rocks.

This method of dating depends on the observation that radioactive elements break down at a steady rate, eventually producing stable 'daughter' elements which are not radioactive. If a rock contains a radioactive element, its age can be estimated by measuring the amount of that element present, plus the amounts of its daughter elements. Advocates of a young earth criticize this dating method on two counts.

Firstly, they question the assumption that radioactive decay has always gone on at the same rate. After all, 'old earth' advocates criticize 'young earthers' for assuming a steady rate of decrease in the strength of the earth's magnetic field. The argument cuts both ways! The response of 'old earth' advocates is that in this case there is reasonable ground for the extrapolation. Nuclear physicists think they know why some atoms are radioactive; their theory that explains this also indicates that radioactive decay should be a steady process. Of course, the theory may eventually be shown to be wrong but, at the moment, it seems valid. In addition, it is pointed out that some radioactive dating techniques (the 'isochron' methods) do not depend on the assumption of regular decay; they are, rather, a way of proving that the decay is regular. Finally, it has been suggested that factors such as extreme temperatures or the level of cosmic radiation might affect the rate of radioactive decay. They clearly do not, however, since rocks from the moon and meteorites give the same ages as those from the earth.

Secondly, 'young earth' advocates make much of the discordant results sometimes obtained from rock samples. Here they point out a real weakness in the method. For example, the daughter elements produced by the decay might get washed out of the rock by water. Most such problems, however, would result in the date obtained being too young, not too old. Also, it is possible to check whether this kind of thing has occurred and make some allowance for it. Opponents of radioactive dating are not always fair in their treatment of discordant results (this is so in the book by Mitchell referred to above). It is still quite common to find them referring to the case of the dating of some lava which gave an age that was clearly too high. However, few of them point out that there is a reasonable explanation for this. The molten lava flowed over much older rock, breaking off bits which were then trapped in the lava when it cooled. When the original samples were taken for dating, this was not realized. Once it had been, it was quite easy to separate out the two types of rock and then sensible results were obtained.

Radioactive dating does have its problems, but the majority of people who have studied the technique think it is unlikely to give rise to errors as great as tenfold. Even that margin of error would not be great enough to make the difference between 10,000 and 10,000 million years.

The fossil record

How is the presence of fossils to be explained if the earth is only 10,000 years old? It is not just the fact of fossils that needs explanation. They occur in distinct groups, and the order in which these groups appear in the rock strata seems to be a fixed one.

The geologic column: an invention?

The arrangement of these various groups in a fixed order is called a geologic column. It can be used to give the relative dates of rock strata: group A, for instance, always appears deeper than group B, and therefore presumably occurred earlier than group B.

It is sometimes said that the geologic column was invented by evolutionists to support their theory. This is quite untrue historically. The first person to develop the geologic column was William Smith. If he were alive now, he would be described as a 'young earth' creationist. However, he lived at the end of the eighteenth century, long before evolution was an issue. He was a geological surveyor involved in mining, canal-digging and road-building. In the course of his work he realized that certain fossils always occurred together. Moreover, in places where several undisturbed strata lay on top of one another, the different fossil groups always appeared in the same order. In any one place, only part of the geologic column is found, but it is not too difficult to build up the whole picture. If in one place the sequence of fossil types is ABCDE, in another DEFGHIJ and in a third HIJKLM, and so on, one can reasonably deduce the whole sequence. There are some places where the sequence is out of order, but these can usually be explained as the result of erosion removing some layers before others were laid down over them, or as the result of major earth movements such as earthquakes.

The fossil sequence: caused by the flood?

The 'young earth, flood geology' position is so called because it maintains that the fossils and the fossil sequence are a result of Noah's flood. Advocates of this position regard the flood as a major, world-wide catastrophe (we will discuss this view of it later) and believe that the fossil sequence can be explained on the basis of three factors:

1. *Hydraulic sorting*. As they drowned in the flood, it would have been the denser and more streamlined creatures which would sink to the bottom of the water first.

However, some particularly large, dense and reasonably streamlined creatures, such as turtles, are never found in the lowest rock strata, while ammonoids – shellfish which are light because their shells have buoyancy chambers full of air – are found there.

2. *Differential mobility*. The more mobile creatures would have been able to flee to higher ground and so would have been drowned last. So dinosaurs were buried before the fleeter mammals.

This does, however, leave some problems. In the lower layers we would expect to find some fossil remains of those mammals that were sleeping, sick, injured or got trapped in their burrows as the flood waters rose. But this is not the case. We would also expect that fossilized remains of pterodactyls, which could fly, would appear in layers higher than the dinosaurs but, again, this is not the case.

3. *Ecological zoning.* Flood geologists argue that the layers of fossils, such as those in the Grand Canyon, represent different ecological zones from the seabed to the uplands, which were inundated in succession.

The problem with this argument is that it provides no explanation for why the layers lie above one another in one place, when the uplands would have been tens of hundreds of miles away from the seashore.

Moreover, none of these three theories accounts for the distribution of plant fossils.

Flood geologists may well be able to refine their theories so that they are more convincing, but much work remains to be done. We will return to some wider aspects of this subject when we discuss the flood story.

This discussion of the age of the earth and of flood geology may seem to have been rather negative. This may reflect my own prejudice. However, the advocates of a 'young earth, flood geology' insist that their position is a scientific one, and I hope that the points made about it above are the result of submitting it to scientific scrutiny. These points have all been made in more specialist scientific literature, but little of it seems to have come through to the wider Christian public. The books of the 'young earth' writers are, however, readily available in most Christian bookshops.

Evolution: the origin of life?

The 'young earth' position is not the only anti-evolutionary one. Many of those who take the 'concordist' interpretation of Genesis 1, which we will discuss later, also reject evolution. Before turning to their view, we will look at some of the criticisms of evolution.

Life does not happen spontaneously

Darwin did not claim to have explained the origin of life, only the origin of species. For many people today, however, the theory of evolution includes the idea of life arising spontaneously on earth from non-living matter.

Some who oppose this aspect of evolutionary theory argue that Pasteur's law of biogenesis 'forbids' life arising spontaneously from non-living matter. Pasteur was fighting the idea that disease-carrying organisms grew spontaneously from dirt. He argued that they could only grow from one another. So if something, perhaps milk, is heated to kill all the disease organisms ('pasteurized') and then kept sealed so that air, which carries the organisms, cannot get at it, it will remain free of them. He proved this to be the case.

However, to say that his law of biogenesis (that disease organisms grow from each other and do not arise spontaneously from non-living matter) 'forbids' the idea that life arose spontaneously on earth is to misunderstand the nature of scientific laws, as we saw in chapter 2. They are *descriptions* of what has been observed to happen under certain conditions; they do not say what *must* happen. Moreover, Pasteur was dealing with organisms that exist today and in today's conditions. Somewhat different organisms might have been able to arise from non-living matter under the different conditions existing on the earth long ago.

Natural processes always lead to greater disorder

A second argument that is put forward against this aspect of evolutionary theory, and indeed the whole concept of evolution, appeals to the Second Law of Thermodynamics. This law is often presented as saying that natural processes always lead to greater disorder ('increased entropy'). It is therefore argued that complex living organisms could not arise by natural processes because their structure is highly ordered (they have low entropy).

This is an over-simple application of the law. The law applies only to a 'closed system' near equilibrium. A closed system is one which cannot exchange energy with its surroundings. The earth is not closed in this sense. It constantly receives energy from the sun. Entropy can decrease on earth without violating the second law provided it increases in the sun (which it does as the sun loses energy). Also, the law only applies to processes close to equilibrium. Fairly recently it has been shown that a system that is far from equilibrium, and able to take in energy, can spontaneously produce order. This has led to a whole new field of 'non-equilibrium thermodynamics'. Some scientists are now investigating such systems in the hope of finding clues to how life might have arisen on earth (we will return to this subject later).

If they succeed, would God become redundant as Creator? Not at all. It is still necessary to explain how it is that matter and the laws of thermodynamics are such that life could arise in this way. The most that can be said is that scientists may have discovered what processes God put into action when, as Genesis says, he commanded the earth to produce life.

God creates instantaneously

Some Christians are not happy with the kind of statement that speaks of God putting 'processes' into action. They argue that 'creation' has to be an instantaneous, miraculous, act. This is not, however, what the Bible actually states. Moreover, in some places God is spoken of as 'creating' something over a period of time, for example, in Isaiah 43:1, 15 God is called the 'creator' of Israel, the same Hebrew word for 'create' being used as in Genesis 1. But the creation of Israel happened over a matter of centuries, from Abraham to Moses. Similarly, the creation of Adam is not presented as an instantaneous act but as a process involving two or three separate stages. This is also the case with the creation of Eve.

Having said all that, it must be added that in fact scientists have not got very far in their attempts to explain how life might have arisen spontaneously on earth. It used to be thought that the atmosphere on the early earth contained hydrogen, methane, ammonia, nitrogen and water. It has been shown that when electrical sparks (lightning?) are put through such a mixture, amino-acids, the building-blocks of the proteins needed for life, are produced. However, geologists now believe that the atmosphere on the early earth was quite different from this and was probably made up of different gases (carbon dioxide, water and a little oxygen), which would not produce amino-acids.

It has also been pointed out that the early earth would have lacked the protective atmosphere it now has. As a result, the intensity of cosmic rays and ultra-violet light reaching the surface would have been enough to destroy the chemical compounds that are the building-blocks of living organisms.

Some scientists are so sceptical of the possibility of life being able to arise on earth that they have suggested that it reached earth from outer space, perhaps via meteorites (see F. Hoyle and N. Wickramasinghe, *Evolution from Space*).

My own conclusion is that claims that life could, or must, have arisen spontaneously on earth are at the moment largely no more than statements of faith in a hypothesis that has little scientific evidence to support it. Of course, more evidence may eventually come to light.

Can we believe Genesis today?

There are two lines of investigation that, at the moment, seem as if they might produce relevant evidence.

The first is the discovery by radio astronomers of the existence of important organic chemicals in interstellar dust clouds. Laboratory experiments are beginning to show how these can form in those clouds. Such chemicals could have been brought to the earth early in its history by the space debris that is constantly bombarding the earth.

The other interesting line of study is the investigation of the simple life-forms which live around the hot water vents that occur in the deep oceans. Before they were discovered, scientists had already concluded that the bacteria which live in hot springs on the earth's surface are some of the most ancient organisms still in existence. Suggestions are now being put forward as to how this type of bacteria might have come into being as a result of the chemical reactions that occur near deep-ocean hot vents.

Evolution: the origin of species?

The theory of evolution is far too big a topic to discuss at length in this book. All we can do is mention briefly a few of the major objections to it and the responses to them.

Missing links in the fossil record

One of the most telling areas of attack on evolution has been the fossil evidence. Darwin admitted that the fossil evidence which, to some extent, seemed to support his theory, also posed problems for it. He was worried about the absence of transitional forms between the separate species, genera and so on. He was also worried by the sudden appearance of the main divisions of animals in the earliest rocks. He hoped that as the study of fossils advanced the problems would disappear. However, Steve Jones, a strong advocate of evolution, has recently written:

> The fossil record – in defiance of Darwin's whole idea of gradual change – often makes great leaps from one form to the next. Far from the display of intermediates to be expected from slow advance through natural selection, many species appear without warning, persist in fixed form, and disappear, leaving no descendants. Geology assuredly does not reveal any finely graded organic chain, and this is the most obvious and gravest objection which can be urged against the theory of evolution (*Almost Like a Whale*, p. 207).

Taken in isolation, this might seem a damaging admission. However, Jones goes on to explain in considerable detail why it is not, for two main reasons.

The first is that fossilization is in fact a very rare event. A variety of conditions have to be just right for it to occur. As a result, one would expect the fossil record to be, as Jones puts it, like 'a series of snap-shots, taken at long intervals with a badly focused camera', which have then been 'faded, torn, stained, lost and muddled by the passage of time'. What is surprising is not the existence of many gaps in the record, but the fact that a fair number of transitional forms *have* been found.

Secondly, the way in which evolution is now understood to work indicates why intermediate forms are rarely found. For example, it has been argued that evolution may proceed best in small groups of creatures which are under ecological stress. In a small group genetic mutations (changes in the hereditary material passed from parents to offspring) are more likely to be preserved and spread due to inbreeding. If the group is under stress (e.g. prey to a fast-running killer) any advantageous change (e.g. ability to run faster, better camouflage) would have immediate effect and so be even more rapidly established. So, it is argued, evolution occurred in situations where few transitional forms would be left, because it involved few creatures and happened in rapid (geologically speaking) spurts.

Opponents of evolution have sometimes pointed to fossils that are out of place as a way of trying to discredit the fossil evidence. The best-known example of this has been the so-called man tracks amongst dinosaur footprints in the Paluxy River bed in Texas. However, J. Morris, one of the popularizers of this evidence, has now, to his credit, admitted that the 'human' tracks are either badly formed dinosaur footprints or simply the result of rock erosion. However, there are still references in books like Mitchell's to a supposed 'shod human footprint' containing crushed trilobites. This is despite the fact that competent geologists who have examined it are sure that it is nothing more than the result of a natural fracturing of the rock called 'spalling', which has left a hollow shaped rather like the sole of a sandal.

Small changes, not large ones

Most anti-evolutionists accept that small changes do occur and even that new species can arise as a result of genetic mutations and natural selection. What they do not accept is that this could lead to major changes. Here they make two main points. Firstly, we have no evidence that major changes have happened (which is true if the fossil evidence is discounted as too debatable). Secondly, it is inconceivable that a major organ could undergo change (e.g a hand becoming a wing) without passing through a stage in which it would be a major disadvantage to the creature concerned.

Evolutionists admit the first point, but add that this is inevitably the case since major changes take a long time. They reply to the second by saying that the problem lies in their opponents' understanding of how evolution proceeds. Evolutionists conceive of such a change taking place by a series of very small steps, each change either making no difference or giving a small advantage to the creature. Some evolutionists lay a lot of stress on what they call 'neutral mutations', which have little or no effect. These, they argue, can build up until some change in the environment results in them producing an important advantage. One of the difficulties for the non-expert is that modern genetics is a highly mathematical discipline which is not easy to understand.

In 1994 *The Proceedings of the Royal Society of London* published a study which presented a possible model of how the focused-lens eye, such as humans have, could have evolved by gradual steps from a light-sensitive patch (which a number of creatures do have). Many of the proposed intermediate forms do in fact exist in various animals today. They estimated that the change would take place in about 364,000 generations. That is a very small fraction of the history of the earth if it is indeed 4,500 million years old.

Natural selection seems cruel and wasteful
Another argument against evolution is not a scientific one but is moral and theological. It is argued that the process of natural selection is cruel and wasteful and is unworthy of a good God. Christian evolutionists agree that there is no simple answer to this problem, any more than there is a simple answer to the question why God allows the

existence of evil and seems to be slow in eradicating it. However, they do suggest two lines of argument that go some way towards dealing with the problem.

In the first place, they point out that whether something is wasteful or not depends on the end-product of a process. Simply to whittle away at a piece of wood until nothing is left but wood shavings might well be considered wasteful. However, if the end-product was a pile of wood shavings and also a beautifully carved Welsh love-spoon, most people would not consider that the wood had been wasted, even if most of it had ended up as shavings. God is the craftsman of the universe, and we must allow him to decide what is the best way to produce the end result he desires and whether or not it is wasteful. Moreover, the 'shavings' of evolution, the species that became extinct, were in fact creatures which had a value and purpose in the eyes of their Creator while they existed.

Secondly, Christian evolutionists argue that there is often more sentiment than real thought involved in this argument. It is certainly wrong for humans to abuse animals (and plants), cause them unnecessary suffering or kill them wantonly. This is because we are moral beings answerable to God for the way we treat his creation, of which he has made us stewards. As far as we know, animals have no moral sense (though some argue that there is evidence of a rudimentary moral sense in the higher primates) and so we cannot apply moral categories to the way they treat each other. Also, since we do not know what goes on in the minds of prey and predator or of an injured animal, it is not clear how terms such as 'cruelty' or 'suffering' can be used of them. We may be transferring our reactions to them illegitimately. However, this is clearly a problematic area for Christians who accept the idea of evolution.

A final comment

G. F. Wright, who was an original 'fundamentalist' in the sense that he contributed to the pamphlets *The Fundamentals*, from which the term derives, said about evolution (see C. A. Russell, *Cross-Currents* [Leicester: IVP, 1985], p. 163):

> If only the evolutionists would incorporate into their system the sweetness of the Calvinistic doctrine of Divine Sovereignty, the church would make no objection to their speculations.

Wright was willing to accept the idea of evolution as a God-directed process.

A lot more could be said both for and against the theory of evolution. Later we will look at the debate over the possible evolutionary origin of the human race. It ought to be clear from what we have said that the question of evolution is not easily resolved, either scientifically or theologically. There is room for legitimate disagreement about it among Christians.

Further reading

R. Dawkins, *Climbing Mount Improbable* (London: Penguin, 1997). A clear exposition of the neo-Darwinian understanding of natural selection. Chapter 5 discusses the evolution of the eye at length.

F. Dyson, *Origins of Life* (Cambridge: Cambridge University Press, 1999). A fairly accessible survey of current scientific ideas about the origin of life on earth.

A. Hayward, *Creation and Evolution: Facts and fallacies*, rev. ed. (London: Triangle, 1994). As an 'old earth creationist' Hayward critiques both 'young earth creationism' and evolution. In particular he provides a detailed critique of many of the arguments for a 'young earth'.

F. Hoyle and N. Wickramasinghe, *Evolution from Space* (London: Dent, 1981). The classic statement of this hypothesis.

S. Jones, *Almost Like a Whale: 'The Origin of Species' updated* (London: Doubleday, 1999). A very readable re-presentation of Darwin's original arguments in the light of the mass of scientific discoveries since *On the Origin of Species* was written.

A. McIntosh, *Genesis for Today: Showing the relevance of the creation/evolution debate to today's society* (Epsom: Day One, 1997). Appendix B has a short report of R. Humphreys' proposals regarding the decay of the earth's magnetic field. It does not take into account the data from pottery.

C. Mitchell, *The Case for Creationism* (Grantham: Autumn House Ltd, 1995). A compendium of arguments in support of 'young earth, flood geology' creationism. It needs to be read in the light of Hayward's book (above) since often Mitchell does not deal with the objections to these arguments which Hayward documents.

R. L. Numbers, *The Creationists: The Evolution of Scientific Creationism* (New York: Knopf, 1992). An excellent, sympathetically written, history of 'young earth' creationism.

D. A. Young, *Christianity and the Age of the Earth* (Grand Rapids, MI: Zondervan, 1982). Arguments in support of an 'old earth' by a professional geologist who is an evangelical Christian.

5
Beginnings: other approaches

Concordist approaches to Genesis 1:1 – 2:3

A number of suggestions have been made about how
Genesis 1 might be interpreted in a way that is in accord
with the findings of modern science. These have been
concerned mainly with the evidence for the great age of
the earth and the existence of the fossils, rather than with
the theory of evolution. They have been labelled
'concordist' interpretations of Genesis 1. Many, if not
most, concordists have rejected evolution. We will deal
briefly with only three examples of this kind of approach.

A gap in creative activity

The 'gap' or 'restitution' theory was first put forward at
the end of the eighteenth century. It was prompted by the
need to explain the growing evidence for a long history of
life on earth provided by the fossil record. It was quite

popular in conservative Christian circles throughout the latter part of the nineteenth century and the early part of the twentieth. This was helped by the fact that Scofield adopted it in his widely used *Reference Bible*. According to this theory, Genesis 1:1 refers to the original creation of the earth. The earth then suffered ruin and destruction, as a result of the rebellion and fall of Lucifer and some of the angels. To accord with this, Genesis 1:2 has to be translated, 'The earth *became* formless and void.' The rest of the chapter can then be read as the restitution of the earth by God in six days of twenty-four hours. All but the most recent rock strata and all the fossils are relegated to the original, ruined creation.

There are at least two major problems with this theory.

For one thing, it rests a major piece of teaching on a fairly rare meaning for the form of the Hebrew verb 'to be' that is used in Genesis 1:2, and on an unusual interpretation of the form of Hebrew grammatical construction used here.

Secondly, there is no clear statement elsewhere in the Bible that the fall of the angels had a ruinous effect on the earth. Attempts to find a hint of it in Isaiah 24:1 and Jeremiah 4:23–26 depend on what most scholars would see as very dubious interpretations.

The 'days' were 'ages'

A number of 'age-day' interpretations of Genesis 1 have been proposed. Their common factor is that the 'days' of creation are taken figuratively, representing successive ages – unspecified periods of many millions of years each. There has been a great deal written about whether or not the Hebrew word for 'day' (*yôm*) can be used in a non-literal way. Much of this is beside the point. It is not just the word 'day' that has to be considered. In its strongest form the age-day interpretation takes the whole week of Genesis 1 to be a metaphorical week, a form of picture language. The creative activity of God over millions of years is pictured as if it were the activity of a normal working week. Some argue that the metaphorical nature of the language is indicated by what is said of the seventh day. There is no mention of 'evening and morning', implying that it has still not ended. This non-literal view of the seventh day also seems required by what Jesus says in John 5:17, which depends for its force on the assumption that we are still in the 'sabbath' of creation week. Exodus 20:11 presents no problem to this interpretation. It says no more than that the pattern of the human week is to be based on the pattern of the divine week of seven creative ages used (metaphorically) in the creation story.

Supporters of the age-day view point out that there is a general agreement between the order of the creative acts and the geological and fossil evidence, though the correspondence is not exact. For example, contrary to the fossil evidence, trees appear before the marine creatures, and birds before insects (if they are included in verse 25). Above all, of course, evening and morning appear before the sun and moon. The last point is often met by saying that the account describes things as they would have appeared to someone on the earth. We are to understand that the sun, moon and stars were created when light was created. They only became visible from the surface of the earth when the clouds, which probably shrouded the earth for much of its history, cleared – perhaps partly due to the effect of plants on the composition of the atmosphere. Other difficulties are explained as the result of the account being concise and therefore partly topical. For instance, all the plants are mentioned together at the time when plants were first created. Critics of this interpretation claim that these arguments seem more like evasions of the problem than explanations of them.

Days of revelation

A third type of interpretation argues that the days of Genesis 1 are days of twenty-four hours, but that they are not the days when God carried out the acts of creation. They are 'revelatory days' when he revealed his work of creation to the author of Genesis. How, it is argued, could any human come to know about God's creative activity when no-one was there until it was nearly over? The answer is: only if God revealed it to someone. Genesis 1 gives a (brief) record of the process of *revelation*, which was spread over six literal days. The order of the creative acts is either said to be topical or (in order to relate it to the fossils) a mixture of chronological and topical.

Probably the greatest weakness of this view is that it is not at all clear that Genesis 1 is meant to be read as the account of a process of revelation, rather than the process of creation.

Neither the age-day nor the revelatory-day interpretation is necessarily either pro- or anti-evolution. Both leave open the question of how God brought living things into being out of the earth and the waters.

A literary-cultural approach to Genesis 1:1 – 2:3

When discussing the rules that should guide our interpretation of the Bible, we saw that it is very important to understand what kind of literature we are dealing with. Is

94

it poetry or prose? If it is prose, what kind of prose is it? The final approach to Genesis 1 that we shall deal with takes these questions as its starting-point. It does not assume that Genesis 1 is to be read as literal prose, but asks what evidence there is in the passage itself to help us see what kind of literature it is.

In our discussion of the age-day approach we saw that it seems necessary to take the seventh day of creation in a non-literal way. Might this be an indication that we should do the same with the others? If so, are there other similar indications? From the early Christian centuries onwards, some commentators on the chapter have found evidence for a non-literal reading of it in the fact that it seems to have a structure that makes excellent logical sense but not such good chronological sense.

For example, in the early third century AD Origen, who was a leading Christian scholar of his day, wrote:

> What man of intelligence, I ask, will consider as a reasonable statement that the first and second and the third day, in which there are said to be both morning and evening, existed without sun and moon and stars, while the first day was even without a heaven? (*First Principles*, 4.3).

His question can be answered by saying that God, being omnipotent, could have bathed the earth in light and darkness on a twenty-four hour cycle before the sun was created. However, that does not seem to be a reasonable way for God to have acted, in the light of the fuller biblical revelation of his dealings with the created order. When God does cause nature to depart from its normal pattern, performing a miracle, it is possible to see good reason for it. Since the time of Origen, it has seemed to many Christians more likely that the apparent 'unreasonableness' in Genesis 1 is to be taken as a pointer to the creation account being non-chronological, topical and theological, than as a pointer to God creating day and night miraculously for the first three days.

The pattern that has been discerned in Genesis 1:1 – 2:3 since the early Christian writers onwards is set out in Figure 3. When first created, the earth is said to be shapeless and empty. The first three days deal with its shape, and the second three with filling it up with creatures suitable to its different parts. The two series of

The earth was

shapeless	and	**empty**
Day 1 The separation of light and darkness.		*Day 4* The creation of the lights to rule the day and the night.
Day 2 The separation of the waters to form the sky and the sea.		*Day 5* The creation of the birds and fish to fill the sky and sea.
Day 3 The separation of the sea from the dry land and creation of plants.		*Day 6* The creation of the animals and humans to fill the land and eat the plants.

Day 7

The heavens and the earth were finished and God rested.

Figure 3 *The structure of Genesis 1:1 – 2:3*

days parallel one another beautifully. The whole structure of the passage reflects and speaks of the order, harmony and beauty of God's creation (the word 'good' in Hebrew has as one of its senses 'beautiful'). God is presented as a good craftsman, and so perhaps the 'week' here is meant to be no more than a figure of speech, which comes naturally to mind when speaking of the work of a craftsman. It is suggested, then, that the purpose of the passage is to speak of the nature of God's creative activity and its outcome, not the details of how he went about it. Hence to ask of it the kind of questions which interest modern science is to ask the wrong kind of question, and to get a wrong answer.

Understanding the literature

It is often said that Genesis 1 is not Hebrew poetry. This is true in the strict sense. However, neither is it simple prose. It has some of the features of Hebrew poetry, such as repetition of phrases, parallelism and carefully balanced phraseology; moreover, even in English translation there is a rhythmic quality about it that is not there in simple prose. This arises because many words and phrases in the passage are repeated three, seven or ten times. Here is a list of some of them (these are not always clear in English translations):

Phrases that occur ten times:
- 'God said' (three times concerning humans, seven times concerning other things);
- creative commands (three times 'Let there be ...', and seven times 'Let');
- 'to make';
- 'according to their kind'.

97

Phrases that occur seven times:
- 'and it was so';
- 'and God saw that it was good'.

Three times it is said that:
- God blessed;
- God created;
- God created men and women.

Other numerical patterns:
- The introduction (1:1–2) contains twenty-one words in Hebrew (three times seven), and the conclusion (2:1–3) contains thirty-five words (five times seven);
- 'Earth' is mentioned twenty-one times and 'God' thirty-five times.

All of this, it is argued, points to an author who is primarily concerned with symbolism (in this case the symbolism of numbers) and so perhaps not concerned (or inspired) to give an exact chronological account.

Another pointer to a non-literal understanding of the passage is the Hebrew word used for 'firmament'. It indicates something that is spread out by hammering, like beaten metal. Job 37:18 speaks of the skies being spread out 'hard as a molten mirror'. In those days mirrors were usually made of polished metal. This suggests that the dome of the sky is being depicted as a dome of beaten metal. In Calvin's terms this is the 'language of appearance', and is to be taken figuratively.

Understanding the cultural setting

To this literary argument for taking the passage in a non-literal way is added a cultural argument. This arises from another of the rules of interpretation that we considered: the need to understand what it would have meant to the original writer and readers. Study of the ideas of creation that were around in the Near East in Old Testament times throws much light on Genesis 1. We will look at this in more detail later but will give a couple of examples now.

Firstly, why are the sun and moon not called by their names, but only referred to as 'lights'? There are perfectly good, common words for sun and moon in Hebrew.

The probable answer is that, in the Semitic languages, of which Hebrew is one, the words 'sun' and 'moon' are also the names of gods. The peoples around the Hebrews worshipped the heavenly bodies as gods and goddesses. Genesis 1:14–19 is an attack on all such thinking. The heavenly bodies are simply 'lights' (just like great big oil lamps!) created by the God of Israel to serve humans (not for humans to serve!) as calendar-markers.

Secondly, the Hebrew verb *bārā'* ('to create'), which in the Old Testament is used only of God's creative activity, occurs three times in the story, in verses 1, 21 and 27. It seems understandable that it should be used in the initial statement about God's creative work in verse 1 and of the final act (the creation of humans) in verse 27. But why is it used in verse 21?

The only convincing answer has to do with the significance of sea monsters in one of the creation stories of Babylon (and probably Canaan too). Here the creator god has to subdue the forces of chaos, depicted as sea monsters, before creating the heavens and the earth. Genesis 1 rejects this by stressing that the sea monsters are just part of God's creation. He did not have to fight and subdue them, he made them!

It is argued that the more closely one looks at Genesis 1

in the light of the religious ideas with which the Hebrews had to do battle, the clearer it is that the meaning of the passage is essentially theological, not historical or scientific. It deals with the questions which theology asks, not those which science asks.

Those theological questions are just as relevant today as they were 3,000 years ago. They are more important than the scientific questions, since they go to the heart of the meaning and purpose of the universe in a way that science cannot.

There is a further consideration. If a literal interpretation of the passage runs into problems with the evidence concerning the age of the earth, the fossils and so on, it may be because the nature of the literature and language has been misunderstood. The evidence of the two 'books' of God's revelation in nature and Scripture ought not to be at cross-purposes.

There are four main criticisms of this literary-cultural approach. Firstly, some literalists regard it as too subtle. They argue that their reading of Genesis 1 is much simpler and more obvious. However, what is simple and obvious depends on the way you approach something. The literalists are open to the charge of being more concerned with what is simple and obvious to them, rather than with what would have been simple and obvious to the first readers or hearers of Genesis 1:1 – 2:3. The real issue is how well the rules of interpretation are being applied.

Secondly, it is argued that recognition of the literary artistry and form of Genesis 1:1 – 2:3 does not necessarily rule out the possibility that it is an account of actual events. There is some validity in this point. However, if it is right to conclude, for the reasons given above, that the 'creation week' was intended as a literary figure of speech, a metaphorical way of presenting God's creative work, then there is no basis in biblical exegesis for taking it as a literal account of an actual chronological series of events. Metaphors are not meant to be taken literally, because they are a form of 'picture language'.

Thirdly, it is argued that seeing in the creation account an attack on the ideas about creation which were common in the culture of the Ancient Near East does not rule out a literal interpretation of the account. Again, there is validity in this point. However, the culturally specific nature of the passage should make us very cautious about reading it as if it was written to address our culture and its (scientific) concerns in a straightforward way. In so far as it addresses theological concerns that have been of relevance to all people at all times, the account does address our culture fairly directly, as we shall see.

Finally, and somewhat related to the previous point, an objection that is sometimes raised against the literary-cultural approach is that it largely ignores the questions raised by science. The answer given to this is that the problem lies in the exaggerated importance our modern culture gives to science and scientific truth. The questions dealt with by Genesis are in fact the more relevant ones, even in our culture.

A pause for thought

It is too early in our study to come to definite conclusions about the different approaches to Genesis 1. The literal and literary-cultural approaches, as outlined in this and the previous chapter, can also be applied to the rest of Genesis 1 – 11. Whether or not they make good sense there too will obviously influence what we think of their application to chapter 1.

Can we believe Genesis today?

Our study of Genesis 1:1 – 2:3 has, however, highlighted three issues.

Firstly, the method of interpretation is the most fundamental issue. It seems that the more literalistic approaches are too simplistic, because they do not take all the rules of good interpretation seriously enough. They generally *assume* that Genesis 1:1 – 2:3 is to be read as simple prose and as addressed directly to the concerns of twenty-first-century people. Those who adopt such an approach do not take the time and effort needed to look at the passage through the eyes of the ancient Israelites to whom it was first addressed. As a result, the light that our knowledge of the literature and culture of the Ancient Near East can throw on how we should understand it is ignored. The literary-cultural approach seems to be a sounder method of interpretation and makes good sense of the passage.

The second issue is the age of the earth. The literalistic interpretation of Genesis comes into head-on conflict with the age of the earth as scientists have determined it by a number of independent methods – all of which produce an answer of several thousand million years. It is my experience that most Christian geologists find the 'scientific' arguments for a young earth scientifically unsound. This is true even of those who, like Davis Young (see his book *Christianity and the Age of the Earth* listed at the end of the last chapter), are anti-evolution.

Having looked briefly at the problems in some arguments for a young earth in the previous chapter, we ought to look briefly at one or two pieces of positive evidence that count against a 'young earth' but which are not often mentioned.

In Wyoming, Utah and Colorado, there are widespread deposits of a rock called the Green River Shale. This consists of hundreds of thousands of fine bands, alternating light and dark in colour. This is typical of sediments laid down in a deep lake. The dark-colour band is the result of the annual washing of organic debris into the lake. This rock, then, records hundreds of thousands of years of sedimentation in a lake. Moreover, the thickness of the bands varies in a periodic way, showing a maximum thickness about every eleven and a half years. This fits with the sunspot cycle, which is known to affect rainfall, and so the amount of material that would be washed into the lake. Some have argued that the occurrence of fossils embedded in several layers of the shale contradicts the interpretation of the layers as annual deposits, because the dead creatures would have decayed too quickly to have been preserved by a covering of silt that took some years to build up. This is not the case. Modern investigations of such lakes show that carcasses which get washed into deep water are protected from decay by the relatively high mineral content and lack of oxygen in the bottom layers of the lake.

Ever since it was realized that the tides are caused by the gravitational pull of the moon and the sun on the water in the oceans, scientists have been aware that the friction produced by the tides as they move around the globe must be slowing the rotation of the earth. The accuracy of modern atomic clocks enables us to measure the rate at which it is slowing. At present the length of the day is increasing by about one second every 50,000 years. The length of the year is not changing because there is virtually no friction of any kind to slow down the earth in its movement around the sun. There are some species of coral and shell fish which show both annual and daily growth bands. Certain fossil corals and shell fish, coming from what are called Devonian rocks, show about 400 daily bands within the annual ones. This fits with the dating of the Devonian rocks to about 400 million years ago by the use of radioactive dating techniques.

There are mats of bacteria, called stromatolites, which grow on the seabed. They, too, show a pattern of both daily and annual growth layers. Fossilized stromatolites from pre-Cambrian rocks show 425 daily bands within the annual ones. This agrees quite well with the dating of the rocks to about 650 million years ago.

The third issue worth highlighting is that the theory of evolution is not compatible with a literal interpretation of Genesis 1. It seems that most Christians involved in the 'life sciences' are unconvinced by the arguments against evolution, though they accept that they do raise some searching questions about it. The attempts to use the flood to explain the fossil evidence do not seem very satisfactory. Apart from the literal interpretation of Genesis, there is no strong theological reason for denying the possibility that God used an evolutionary process to bring into existence the life-forms he wanted.

The literary-cultural approach is not directly affected by the scientific arguments about the age of the earth and evolution. This is because it leads to the conclusion that the message of Genesis 1:1 – 2:3 is theological rather than scientific. (We will look at that theological message in some detail in a later chapter.) It concentrates on the nature of God and the world he created, and his purposes in creating it. The questions of *how* he did it is left open.

This should not surprise us in view of what we have seen earlier about the relationship between scientific and religious truth. The 'how?' questions are the legitimate concern of scientists. We have seen that their answers should not be rejected lightly. If they do conflict with our understanding of what the Bible says, then we should think seriously about the soundness of our method of interpretation as well as examining the soundness of the scientific claims. The 'rules of interpretation' we have discussed were not drawn up with the problems of Genesis in mind. They are rules which have arisen as a result of applying the results of the study of literature in general to the study of the Bible. The literary-cultural approach to Genesis seems to apply them more carefully and consistently than the literalistic approach does, and this is a decisive point in its favour.

Further reading

H. Blocher, *In the Beginning* (Leicester and Downers Grove, IL: IVP, 1984). A detailed study of Genesis 1 – 3 which favours a non-literalistic interpretation.

N. M. de S. Cameron, *Evolution and the Authority of the Bible* (Exeter: Paternoster, 1983). Argues that the witness of the Bible runs counter to acceptance of evolution.

M. A. Jeeves and R. J. Berry, *Science, Life and Christian Belief* (Leicester: Apollos, 1998). Chapters 6 and 7 argue that there is no conflict between evolution and the biblical revelation.

D. F. Kelly, *Creation and Change* (Fearn, Ross-shire: Mentor, 1999). A study of Genesis 1:1–2:4 which argues for a literal interpretation.

D. Spanner, *Biblical Creation and the Theory of Evolution* (Exeter: Paternoster, 1978). Argues in some detail for the compatibility of an evolutionary understanding of the origin of life and the biblical revelation.

G. J. Wenham, *Genesis 1 – 15*, Word Biblical Commentary (Waco, Texas: 1987). A very good detailed commentary by a leading evangelical scholar.

Can we believe Genesis today?

P. J. Wiseman, *Clues to Creation in Genesis* (London: Marshall, Morgan & Scott, 1977) Argues for the 'revelatory day' interpretation of Genesis 1.

D. A. Young, *Creation and the Flood* (Grand Rapids, MI: Baker, 1977). Argues for a version of the 'age-day' interpretation of Genesis 1.

6
Creation, chaos and design

Having looked at Genesis 1 in some detail, we are going to consider some important general issues concerning science and creation before moving on to Genesis 2 – 11.

An absolute beginning?

On the basis of Hebrew grammar alone it is possible to translate Genesis 1:1–2a in two different ways:

> [1]In the beginning, when God created the universe, [2]the earth was formless and desolate (*The Good News Bible*).

> [1]In the beginning God created the heavens and the earth. [2]Now the earth was formless and empty ...
> (*The New International Version*).

The difference between these translations is that the second begins with nothingness, whereas the first allows the possibility that Genesis 1 begins with something – the existence of unformed matter, to which God then gives form and order. In other words, the first does not speak about the absolute beginning of the universe.

There are several reasons for preferring the second translation.

Firstly, verse 1 speaks of the creation of the earth or, more probably, of everything (the phrase 'the heavens and the earth' is a Hebrew way of saying this, hence the translation 'universe'). It seems strange, then, to take verse 2 as meaning that the earth existed before this.

Secondly, elsewhere the Old Testament implies (e.g. Psalm 33:6–9; Proverbs 8:22–27; Isaiah 48:12–13), and the New Testament states (e.g. Colossians 1:15–17; Hebrews 11:3), that originally God alone existed and that the whole material world was brought into being by him. Therefore it did have an absolute beginning. It seems reasonable to interpret Genesis 1 in harmony with this.

Thirdly, this is how the majority of Jewish scholars (at least since the third century BC) and Christian scholars have understood the passage. It is particularly significant that this is how Jewish scholars understood it in pre-Christian times when Hebrew was still to some degree a living language. They were better placed than we are to judge how to understand this passage.

Creation from nothing?

Related to this issue of interpretation is a scientific one. Most astronomers think that the evidence points to our universe beginning with a kind of explosion of energy, which was also the origin of space and time. Some scientists imply that, since it now seems possible (though not yet certain) that the 'big bang' can be explained as arising from fluctuations in a 'quantum vacuum', science explains the ultimate origin of the universe. It does not and, in principle, cannot. A 'quantum vacuum' is not absolute nothingness. It is a kind of force field or energy field. Science has not explained the existence of such a 'vacuum', nor why it should have such characteristics as to make those fluctuations possible and why they should produce a universe. Any scientific explanation of these matters would have to be in terms of some prior situation or principles, which would then need an explanation, and so on. This is because, as we saw in chapter 2, science aims to give naturalistic explanations of what happens in the material world. It has to assume the existence of some kind of material world. According to the theory of relativity, energy and matter are interchangeable, so a 'quantum vacuum' is a 'material world'. Logically and rationally, one is free either simply to accept the existence of that world without any kind of ultimate explanation for it or to believe (on other than purely scientific grounds) that God created it. Science can never deny the second possibility.

The Christian doctrine that God created the world 'out of nothing' does not mean that the 'nothing' is a kind of 'something' out of which God made the world. It is a shorthand way of saying that matter is not eternal (only God is) and that the world is entirely dependent on God for its existence.

SETI

Did God create only one inhabited planet? This is not a new question, provoked by the 'space age'. It was discussed by the philosophers of ancient Greece – some of whom answered 'Yes' and others 'No'. Some of the early

Can we believe Genesis today?

Christian theologians discussed the question, and concluded that God had created only one inhabited world. This was more because they disagreed with the philosophy of the Greeks, who had argued for many worlds, than for any clearly biblical reason. In the Middle Ages scholars occasionally addressed this question. Thomas Aquinas, one of the most influential medieval theologians, believed that God could have created many inhabited worlds, but concluded that he probably had not. Some Christian scholars of the nineteenth century were prepared to accept that God had created other inhabited planets. Strangely, there has been little discussion of this question by Christians since, until very recently.

Unlike the theologians, since the middle of the twentieth century, scientists have been very interested in the possibility of life on other planets. The theory of evolution, ideas about how life might have arisen from non-living matter, and a growing understanding of how the solar system may have formed have led some to be very optimistic about the likelihood of life on other planets. In 1960 an astronomer, Frank Drake, began a systematic search for radio signals from extra-terrestrial intelligent beings, and so began the Search for Extra-Terrestrial Intelligence (SETI). Forty years on, teams of searchers are still at it, but have yet to register any success.

One of the assumptions made by SETI enthusiasts is that our solar system is a typical one. However, recently evidence to the contrary has been accumulating. Although our telescopes are not powerful enough to look for planets around nearby stars, we can now get indirect evidence of their existence. If a star has a planet orbiting around it, its position in the sky 'wobbles' because the star and the planet both orbit their common centre of gravity, which is not the centre of the star. Sensitive instruments called spectroscopes can detect this wobble, and by measuring its characteristics astronomers can calculate the size of the planet and its distance from the star. A systematic search of nearby (in astronomical terms) sun-like stars has led to the discovery of about ten with planets. Not surprisingly, these are all large – from about half the size of Jupiter, the largest planet in our solar system, to about ten times its size. Large planets cause large 'wobbles' and so are the easiest to find. What has surprised astronomers is that, unlike Jupiter, most of these are orbiting closer to their star than the earth is to the sun, and in some cases closer even than Mercury, the innermost of the planets in our system. This has led them to revise their theories of how planetary systems form, and some have concluded that, far from being a typical system, our solar system may be a 'freak'. If so, the chance of intelligent life existing elsewhere is a lot lower than was previously thought.

All planets, the earth included, wobble as they spin on their axis. With the rise of 'chaos theory' (see below), it became clear that this wobble should sometimes result in major shifts in the direction of the earth's axis of rotation. These would produce major changes in the global climate. This would probably make the development of life on earth by an evolutionary process impossible. However, the earth has not suffered such shifts because the gravitational pull of the moon stabilizes the direction of its axis of rotation. So, a planet needs to have a large moon orbiting around it if it is to be a suitable place for life to evolve. That too lessens the odds of it having happened elsewhere by a natural process.

In 1996 a team of NASA scientists caused a stir by claiming that they had found tiny fossil bacteria in a meteorite from Mars. The validity of that claim is still hotly debated. However, if bacterial life did arise on Mars, it is clear that it did not lead to intelligent life there. One reason for this is that, because Mars has only two very small moons, its axis of rotation has undergone major changes in direction.

What would be the implications for Christian faith if the SETI project should discover that there are other intelligent beings in our universe? The astronomer Paul Davies thinks that it would be a major problem for Christianity, because it would undermine its claim that humans have a special and exclusive relationship with the Creator. He is mistaken in thinking this, because, although Christians believe that humans have a special relationship with God – being made in God's image – there is nothing in the Bible to suggest that this is an *exclusive* relationship. The Bible is silent about the existence of any intelligent life on other planets.

Let us suppose that there is intelligent life elsewhere in the universe. It would be natural to conclude that a loving Creator would establish a personal relationship with those beings as he has done with us. Would they have 'fallen'? We cannot say. If they did, how would God act to save them? Again, we cannot really say. It might depend on the nature of their 'fallenness'.

Christian theologians have made three suggestions. Some have argued, in the light of passages like Colossians 1:15–20 which speak of the 'cosmic' significance of Christ, that the act of atonement achieved on earth is unique and of cosmic significance. Just as the cross is effective across time, being the basis of salvation for those humans who lived before it, so it could be effective across space for beings on other planets. Whether, and how, God would make them aware of it we cannot say. Others have argued that there is no reason why God the Son could not have been incarnated on other planets, in an appropriate

112

form, to make atonement in an appropriate way for other beings. After all, who are we to put limitations on what God can do? There are others who think that all we can say, from our knowledge of God, is that God would do whatever is necessary to save any of his creatures.

However many inhabited planets there may be, presumably God could bring together the culmination of his purposes for all of them in a single great cosmic Day of the Lord when the Creator comes to complete the redemption of the whole of his creation.

God and chance

Some people find another problem in the fact that, in modern scientific thought, 'chance' or 'random' events play an important role in the fundamental process of the universe, from atomic physics to genetics. This seems to raise questions over the traditional Christian teaching about a purposeful creation and divine providence. Jacques Monod, winner of a Nobel prize for his work in molecular biology, claims that chance, not God, is the real creator:

> Chance alone is at the source of every innovation, of all creation in the biosphere. Pure chance, absolutely free but blind, is at the very root of the stupendous edifice of evolution (*Chance and Necessity*, p. 110).

Here Monod makes a classic logical blunder. He treats 'chance' as if it were a positive force or cause, when it is quite the opposite. Scientists use the terms 'chance' and 'random' in a very specific way when referring to events. A chance event is one that cannot be predicted by scientists or can only be predicted in terms of statistical probability. What Monod is saying is really no more than that the genetic mutations that play an important part in evolution are events which scientists cannot predict. This does not mean that they have no cause (some of them are known to be caused by certain chemicals or types of radiation), or that God, if he exists, could not predict them.

A simple analogy may help here. A good spin bowler (all too rare in modern cricket!) will produce a variety of deliveries – the off-spinner, the top-spinner, the arm-ball, the straight ball. He will try to deliver them with little change in his delivery action and in a fairly random pattern. If he is successful, the batsman will not be able to predict what kind of delivery it is until he is in mid-stroke. The batsman's inability to predict the delivery does not mean that the delivery is unplanned and lacking in purpose. What seems random from one point of view may be thoroughly purposeful from another.

We can see, then, that there is no contradiction between the importance of chance in the physical processes of the universe and belief in the providence of God at work in the world. The fact is that the Bible does not hesitate to regard what from a human point of view appear to be chance happenings, as being fully within the purpose of God. (For example, Micaiah the prophet predicted the death of Ahab, caused by an arrow fired at random: 1 Kings 22:17, 34; see also Proverbs 16:33.)

As far as the question of design in nature is concerned, it is worth pointing out that random processes can be used purposefully. Modern designers use computerized 'random search' programmes to do certain design tasks, because they are the quickest and most efficient way of doing them.

The Anthropic Principle

Unlike Monod, who concluded that the appearance of life is a pure accident, over the last twenty years or so a number of astronomers have been arguing that the universe appears to be 'fine-tuned for life'. They have labelled this 'the Anthropic Principle' (*anthropos* is a Greek word meaning man/humankind).

They have come to this view because the existence of complex life in the universe, assuming it arose by a natural process, depends critically on the value of several of the fundamental physical constants. There seems to be no other reason why these constants have the value they do. For example, if gravity were just slightly stronger than it is, the universe would have collapsed in on itself long ago. If it were slightly weaker, stars would never have formed. If the balance between the forces of gravity and electro-magnetism were slightly different, stars would either not exist or would burn out very quickly.

What is the significance of this feature of our universe? Some people just shrug their shoulders and say, 'We are here because we are here.' Some scientists argue that the current form of the 'big bang' theory allows for the existence of millions of universes, and one of them was bound to have the right conditions for life. This appeals to the existence of millions of universes that we cannot ever observe. Others hope that, one day, science will show us that the constants have the value they do for some reason not related to the existence of life. This puts a lot of faith in the progress of science! Christians, of course, can rightly say that the Anthropic Principle fits in well with their understanding of God and the universe. It is evidence of the reasonableness of Christianity, but cannot be used as proof of it.

Chaos theory

In the 1960s scientists discovered a phenomenon which was initially given the name 'chaos'. It began to be written and talked about in the popular media in the 1980s. The choice of name for the phenomenon was unfortunate, because the scientists did not mean by 'chaos' what the word means in everyday English. As Ian Stewart puts it, what scientists mean by chaos is 'apparently lawless behaviour governed entirely by law' (*Does God Play Dice?* [Oxford: Blackwell, 1989], p. 17).

Chaos, in the scientific sense, arises when a physical system becomes very sensitive to tiny changes within it. Scientists may then be unable to predict the behaviour of the system for one, or both, of two reasons. Firstly, the size of the changes which produce major effects may be too small for us to measure with existing instruments. Secondly, even if we can measure them accurately, the degree of accuracy needed in the subsequent calculation to predict what will happen may be such that even the biggest and fastest computers available today would very quickly run out of memory space to do the calculations. In fact, it was the advent of computers which made the discovery and study of chaotic systems possible. So, chaotic systems do not behave 'randomly' in the popular sense of the word. They are governed by the normal laws of nature. The problem is our inability either to obtain or to process the information we need in order to predict their behaviour. Because the behaviour of chaotic systems is complex, scientists are tending more and more to talk about 'complexity theory' rather than 'chaos theory', which is less confusing for the general public, though less headline catching.

It is quite often the case that a system can behave quite

normally but then, as some aspect of it changes, it can quite suddenly change into a state in which it behaves chaotically. Unfortunately for forecasters, this is what happens with weather systems. A system may be quite 'well-behaved' for days or weeks, but, as the pressure or temperature or some other element changes, it can quite suddenly shift into a chaotic pattern of behaviour. The sensitivity of some weather systems when they are in a chaotic state has been called 'the butterfly effect' – the flapping of a butterfly's wing in the Amazon jungle might cause a tornado in Alabama a few days later. Unfortunately, weather forecasters cannot take into account the behaviour of butterflies when doing their forecasts!

A scientist and theologian, John Polkinghorne, has suggested that chaotic systems might provide a means by which God acts in the world in a 'hidden' way. Because of their sensitivity, God would need to influence them only to a very tiny degree to push them in the direction he wanted events to go. This is an interesting idea and might, for example, apply to the appearance of the strong east wind that drove back the Red Sea before the fleeing Israelites. However, it is hard to see how it might apply to other acts of God, such as the use of foreign nations to chastise Israel for her disobedience to the covenant law.

Order out of chaos

An interesting aspect of chaotic, or complex, systems is that in certain circumstances they can, quite spontaneously, become highly ordered. This production of order out of chaos occurs when they are pushed into a state that is far from their normal equilibrium state. The study of these states has opened up the new area of 'non-equilibrium thermodynamics'. It is an area that is too

117

complicated for us to pursue here. However, the discovery of these 'self-organizing' systems, as they are called, is of obvious relevance to the question of the possibility of living cells arising from non-living matter. This could not have happened in a single step, of course, but scientists interested in the origin of life are studying non-equilibrium thermodynamics and self-organizing systems for possible clues to how it might have happened in a series of steps.

Design in nature

During the eighteenth and early nineteenth centuries, the 'argument from design' was very popular with Christians as a way of arguing for the existence of God. In particular, people would point to features of the natural world, such as the human eye, and argue that its complexity and the fact that it functioned so well pointed to its being the product of design by the Creator. This line of argument lost a lot of its force, both because of philosophical criticisms of it and because of Darwin's theory of natural selection, which seemed to undercut it. In recent years it has been revived in somewhat different forms.

Darwin's black box

In the mid-1990s Michael Behe, a biochemist, argued that there are structures and processes in the living cell which are 'irreducibly complex'. He defines what he means by this.

> By irreducibly complex I mean a single system composed of several well-matched, interacting parts that contribute to the basic function, wherein the

removal of any one of the parts causes the system to effectively stop functioning (*Darwin's Black Box*, p. 39).

He gives a number of examples: blood-clotting, the immune response to infection, and the cilia (tiny hair-like structures) which enable bacteria to move in liquids. In his view, such systems cannot be produced by a series of small modifications from simpler systems, because the simpler systems would be non-functional, and so of no use to the living cell. He uses a mousetrap as an example of an irreducibly complex system. It has a number of parts (a base, a sensitive trigger, a bar to crush the mouse, a catch to hold the bar back when the trap is primed), and, if any one is missing, the trap is useless for catching mice.

There have been a number of critical responses to Behe's book. We will not look at those which delve into the details of the biochemistry, except to say that quite a lot of work has been done on some of the systems that he claims are irreducibly complex, which provides pointers to how they may have come into being by gradual processes. Behe does not refer to this work.

One of the telling criticisms is that it is, in fact, not difficult to understand how an irreducibly complex system could be built up gradually by adding parts. Initially, a system (A) may carry out a particular function, perhaps not all that efficiently. A part (B) may then get added because it helps A be rather more efficient. It is not essential, but simply improves things. However, either A or B may then change in such a way that it becomes essential for the two parts to work together. This process can then continue as more parts are added, until the system is quite complex. This is just the kind of process that would be expected from a neo-Darwinian perspective.

Can we believe Genesis today?

Another criticism is that Behe ignores the possibility that although a change in a complex system may result in its no longer fulfilling its original function, it may still have a useful function within the cell. His mousetrap example can be used as a simplistic analogy. Loss of the catch that holds back the bar would make it useless, but it could then be used as a spring-loaded clip to hold papers together – still a useful function in the study in which the trap was originally placed to catch mice. There are some indications that this kind of thing might have happened in the history of the living cell.

There is a phenomenon called 'gene duplication', which makes the modification of irreducibly complex systems possible in cells. When gene duplication occurs, a cell has two genes to produce a certain molecule. One of the genes may then be modified by mutation with the result that a new molecule is produced which has a different function. This happens without the loss of the original function. This, evolutionary biologists suggest, is how myoglobin, which is quite similar to haemoglobin, came into being. Haemoglobin carries oxygen in the blood. Myoglobin carries it in muscles. It could be that myoglobin arose from duplication, and then modification, of the haemoglobin gene.

Intelligent design

Behe is one of a group of scholars who have recently been arguing that the concept of 'intelligent design' ought to have a place within scientific thinking. The theoretical case for this has been worked out in some detail by William Dembski. The full argument is mathematically based, and the attempt to express it in words alone inevitably simplifies it greatly.

When faced with a very unusual set of circumstances, we naturally find ourselves wondering whether it is simply the result of chance or whether someone (an intelligent cause) has been manipulating (designing) the outcome. So, when Ms A finds that she keeps meeting Mr B at unexpected times and places, she begins to wonder whether this is just chance or whether Mr B (or his friend C) is carrying out a plan to bring them together so that they can get to know one another. Dembski is concerned to establish criteria by which an event can justifiably be classified as 'designed'. He rules out events that can be explained as the necessary outcome of the operation of the laws of nature. This leaves events that are, to some extent, the result of chance processes. If an event is to be classified as 'designed', we need to be able to calculate the probability of its occurring by chance, and we need to be able to do this independently of the occurrence of the event itself. We also need to specify what level of improbability is need for us to attribute the event to 'design' rather than simply to chance. Dembski's theoretical analysis seems plausible, but time will tell how plausible it is as it is assessed by those with the mathematical and philosophical ability to do so rigorously. There are, however, at least two areas in which it raises problematic issues.

The first is whether his procedure can in fact be applied in a useful way in science. In his writings Dembski tends to lean on the work of Behe, which, as we have seen, has question marks against it. This seems to lead him to underestimate the difficulty of calculating the improbabilities that his procedure depends on. On one occasion Dembski refers to a calculation presented at a symposium about forty years ago. This concerned the probability of a medium-sized protein coming about by chance. The calculation suggested that this was an astronomically low number. That calculation has been referred to in popular and semi-popular literature ever since. However, knowing what we do now about proteins, it is clear that it was done in a far too simplistic way. One reason for this is that it was assumed that proteins, which are made up of sub-units called amino-acids, are like a long necklace made of different beads put together on a string, and that it was crucial for the different beads to be in exactly the right order. However, we now know that, for some stretches of the 'necklace', the exact order of the beads does not matter. This is because many proteins fold up into a kind of ball. What matters is that on the surface of the ball amino-acids should be water-soluble and that on the inside they should be fat-soluble. This leaves a good deal of freedom as to exactly which amino-acids are found on the inside or outside, and in which order they are arranged on the 'string'. The result is that the calculated probability of the sequence of amino-acids occurring by chance is greatly increased.

The second issue is whether expecting 'gaps' in nature that are inexplicable by science makes good sense biblically and theologically. This leads us into a wider discussion.

God, science and gaps

Orthodox science is based on what is called *methodological naturalism*. What this means is that the only explanations that are acceptable are ones expressed in terms of natural causes. This is not to deny the reality of the 'supernatural' or the possibility of 'miracles' that cannot be explained by natural causes. It simply says that they lie beyond the bounds of science. Unfortunately, there are a few atheistic scientists, such as Richard Dawkins, who seek to claim the methodological naturalism of science as support for their *metaphysical naturalism*. Metaphysical naturalism is the ideological belief that 'nature' is the only reality there is. This claim is illegitimate because, as we saw in chapter 1, modern science grew up in a framework of Christian thought and its success can, to some extent, be taken as a vindication of the Christian assumptions of the early modern scientists. Moreover, methodological naturalism is simply a 'rule of procedure', not a statement about the nature of reality as a whole.

Some Christians are unhappy about the use of methodological naturalism in science. They argue for what they call 'theistic science', namely allowing into science hypotheses about God as a designer and as an agent in the working of the world. This raises all kinds of practical problems. We have seen that it is far from easy to decide when a system is 'irreducibly complex' or when it is 'intelligently designed'. Perhaps, for the good of progress in science, it would be best simply to ignore these possibilities and just get on with looking for naturalistic explanations. Then there are scientists, both Christian and non-Christian, who are concerned that science could be stultified by people too readily taking the short-cut of 'solving' difficult problems by invoking the agency of God rather than looking for natural causes. It might also make science into a battleground for theists and atheists each trying to prove their case, or lead to a separation into two camps of 'theistic' and 'non-theistic' scientists. Far better, they say, for Christians to be able to join with others of all faiths and none in a common enterprise based on a methodology acceptable to all.

The idea that the concept of 'design' necessarily requires that there be gaps in nature which orthodox science cannot bridge – the position adopted by both Behe and

Dembski – is problematic from a theological and biblical perspective. It implies that God is not active or discernible in the 'normal' course of nature. The Bible does not appeal to 'gaps' in nature as evidence of God's existence or power. Instead, it appeals to the wonderful overall pattern that can be seen in God's creation (Psalm 19:1; Romans 1:20). Also, it speaks clearly of God being constantly active in the sustaining of nature (Psalm 104; Colossians 1:17; Hebrews 1:3).

Appealing to God to explain 'gaps' which science cannot explain has proved dangerous in the past. The so-called 'God-of-the-gaps' argument was used quite often as an aspect of the 'design argument' mentioned earlier in this chapter. Unfortunately for those who used it, and for the reputation of God, many of the 'gaps' used in the argument have been closed as science has advanced and so, to the unbeliever, God has seemed to become less and less necessary and belief in God less and less credible. Of course orthodox Christians do assert that there are genuine 'gaps', miraculous events which science cannot explain. However, in the Bible these are not part of the way nature is constituted. Nor are they used as logical proofs of God's existence. To use the language of John's Gospel, they are 'signs' – pointers to God's nature (and so aids to faith) – not proofs of God's existence (which would make faith unnecessary).

Limiting God's activity in the natural world to 'gaps' seems to some not to be 'theistic science' but a move away from biblical theism towards what is called 'deism'. Deism is the belief that God created the world and then left it to run itself, like a wound-up clockwork motor. If God only works in gaps in nature, does nature run itself? If not, and God is active in nature as well, why do there need to be 'gaps'? They would seem to imply that God is incapable of creating nature as a coherent 'gap-free' system which he then upholds. This is surprising if God is all-powerful.

Many Christians who are active in science favour the view that the universe is the creation of a personal, all-powerful, all-wise and faithful God who is distinct from the universe. However, unlike the deists, they believe that God is intimately involved in sustaining every aspect of the creation moment by moment. The 'laws of nature' are expressions of God's 'normal' activity in the world. Sometimes God acts in an 'extraordinary' way, but such actions, by their nature, lie outside the sphere of scientific investigation. Most would go on to say that the 'laws of nature' are not the direct activity of God but the operation of powers and processes which God created and upholds. They have a measure of freedom, but are never left 'unsupervised' in the way the deists would assert. This view has been called 'robust theism'. It is not a new one. Both Augustine of Hippo and Basil of Caesarea, in the fifth century BC, understood the commands beginning 'Let ...' in Genesis 1 not as commands that were obeyed once for all at a single moment, but more as permission, or power, given by God to the earth, the waters and so on, which were to continue in operation down through the ages. The view that creation has been gifted by God with a measure of power within itself to keep operating and developing has been called 'the functional integrity of creation'. If over-pressed it, too, can move towards deism.

Behind the discussion and debate about intelligent design, theistic science, robust theism and the functional integrity of creation, there is the difficulty of envisaging and speaking about how God is active in the physical world. Rather than dividing into warring camps, there is the need for Christians to remain in fruitful dialogue with one another over this issue. The fact is that we are not in a position where we can say that scientists will never find the concept of intelligent design useful. Nor are we in the position to deny the possibility that in the future natural processes will be found to bridge what at the moment seem to be unbridgeable gaps.

Further reading

J. Barrow, *The Origin of the Universe* (London: Phoenix, 1995). An introductory account of current thinking about the big-bang theory.

M. Behe, *Darwin's Black Box* (New York: Free Press, 1996). See the discussion in this chapter.

P. Davies, *Are We Alone?* (London: Penguin, 1995). Subtitled 'Philosophical implications of the discovery of extraterrestrial life'.

W. A. Dembski, *Intelligent Design* (Downers Grove, IL: IVP, 1999). A fairly popular presentation of intelligent-design theory, put within a Christian context.

J. Gleick, *Chaos: Making a new science* (New York: Viking Press, 1987). A very readable account of the origins and development of chaos theory.

J. Houghton, *The Search for God: Can science help?* (Oxford: Lion, 1995). Chapter 5 discusses the 'fine-tuned for life' aspect of the universe.

P. E. Johnson, *Testing Darwinism* (Leicester: IVP, 1997; = *Defeating Darwinism*, Downers Grove, IL: IVP, 1997). A cogent attack on naturalism. Johnson does not seem to understand the difference between metaphysical and methodological naturalism and so, wrongly, asserts that the theory of evolution is naturalistic in the metaphysical sense.

J. Monod, *Chance and Necessity* (London: Collins, 1983). See the discussion in this chapter.

R. T. Pennock, *Tower of Babel* (Cambridge, MA: MIT Press, 1999). Subtitled 'The evidence against the new creationism'. It contains a critique of those like Michael Behe, William Dembski and Philip Johnson who use the idea of intelligent design to challenge evolution.

I. Prigogine and I. Stengers, *Order out of Chaos* (London: Flamingo, 1985). A discussion of non-equilibrium thermodynamics and its significance. A demanding read.

P. D. Ward and D. Brownlee, *Rare Earth* (New York: Copernicus/Springer-Verlag, 2000). Subtitled 'Why complex life is uncommon in the universe'.

D. Wilkinson, *Alone in the Universe?* (Crowborough: Monarch, 1997). Discusses the whole 'alien phenomenon' from a Christian point of view.

D. Wilkinson, *God, the Big Bang and Stephen Hawking*, rev. ed. (Crowborough: Monarch, 1996). A good, readable discussion of the big-bang theory and related issues from a Christian perspective.

7
Puzzles in Genesis 2 – 5

[4]This is the account of the heavens and the earth when they were created.

When the LORD God made the earth and the heavens – [5]and no shrub of the field had yet appeared on the earth and no plant of the field had yet sprung up, for the LORD God had not sent rain on the earth and there was no man to work the ground, [6]but streams came up from the earth and watered the whole surface of the ground – [7]the LORD God formed the man from the dust of the ground and breathed into his nostrils the breath of life, and the man became a living being.

[8]Now the LORD God had planted a garden in the east, in Eden; and there he put the man he had formed. [9]And the LORD God made all kinds of trees grow out of the ground – trees that were pleasing to the eye and good for food. In the middle of the garden were the tree of life and the

tree of the knowledge of good and evil (Genesis 2:4–9).

Some people find these verses puzzling, coming after the creation story in chapter 1. They read a bit like the beginning of another, different creation story.

A contradictory account?

According to some Old Testament scholars, Genesis 2:4–25 contains a second creation story which contradicts that of Genesis 1:1 – 2:3. In chapter 2, they say, man is created before the plants and animals. Also, 2:5 seems to show the early earth as an arid desert, not the watery chaos of 1:2. What can we say about this?

Firstly, when we looked at the 'rules of interpretation', we saw that, if the Bible is inspired by God, who is truth, we would not expect it to contradict itself. This encourages us to look for ways of harmonizing apparent contradictions, provided this can be done without twisting Scripture.

Secondly, even if this were not the case, it would be strange if the author of Genesis simply put two contradictory accounts of creation side by side.

Bearing these two points in mind, it makes good sense to see chapter 1 as a panoramic view of God's creative work, with chapter 2 then focusing in on the climactic work, the creation of human beings. Verses 5 and 6 of chapter 2 can be taken as referring to the state of things in the area where the garden of Eden came into being – arid, but fertile if properly irrigated. The mention of plants being created refers only to the garden of Eden and need not imply that plants did not already exist elsewhere.

Finally, the Hebrew verb used in verse 19 allows it to

mean, 'Now the LORD God *had* formed out of the ground all the beasts of the field ...' (as in the NIV), referring back to an earlier act of creation.

The location of Eden

[10]A river watering the garden flowed from Eden; from there it was separated into four headwaters. [11]The name of the first is the Pishon; it winds through the entire land of Havilah, where there is gold. [12](The gold of that land is good; aromatic resin and onyx are also there.) [13]The name of the second river is the Gihon; it winds through the entire land of Cush. [14]The name of the third river is the Tigris; it runs along the east side of Asshur. And the fourth river is the Euphrates (Genesis 2:10–14).

The location of the garden of Eden, as indicated by these verses, is a matter for debate. There are two main views.

Some think that the description points to a place at the head of the Persian Gulf, where the Tigris and Euphrates met and formed a delta. This view is influenced partly by the identification of Havilah with Arabia, suggested by Genesis 25:18: '[Ishmael's] descendants settled in the area from Havilah to Shur, near the border of Egypt, as you go towards Asshur.' Also, in Babylonian literature paradise is thought of as located in the Persian Gulf. There is some evidence to link the Babylonian paradise with the island of Bahrain.

The other view places Eden in the upland plateaux of what is now eastern Turkey, where the Tigris and Euphrates rise. The other two rivers are then sometimes identified with the Araxes (flowing into the Caspian Sea) and Halys (flowing into the Black Sea). In ancient times gold was found in some of the rivers in the area between the Caspian and Black Seas. The story of Jason's golden fleece relates to this region. The location of Havilah is by no means definitely Arabia. Cush in the Old Testament usually clearly refers to Ethiopia but this cannot be the case in Genesis 2. In Genesis 10:6–10 Cush may mean the Kassite people who lived in western Iran in antiquity. This Cush is also linked with Havilah (10:7), which may therefore have been in the same kind of region.

Both of the locations suggested for Eden had an arid climate in ancient times and we cannot choose between them simply on the basis of Genesis 2:10–14. We will look at this again later.

Interpreting Genesis 2 and 3

Interpretations of Genesis 2 and 3 come in two basic varieties – the 'literal' and the 'literary-cultural'. Those who adopt a 'concordist' approach to Genesis 1 are divided over how to interpret chapters 2 and 3. There are in reality a number of different 'literal' and 'literary-cultural' interpretations, with some lying somewhere between the two extremes. For the sake of clarity of comparison, we will consider the more 'thoroughgoing' examples of each basic variety.

The literal approach

The literal approach to interpretation may seem quite simple and straightforward here, but it does have problems. For instance, are we really to take 2:7 literally, with God forming a dust pile into human form and breathing into it? '... the LORD God formed the man from the dust of the ground and breathed into his nostrils the breath of life, and the man became a living being.' Surely the 'breathing' at least must be metaphorical. God does not have lungs and nostrils as we do.

If we take 2:21–22 literally, we must assume that God behaved as a modern surgeon carrying out an operation:

> So the LORD God caused the man to fall into a deep sleep; and while he was sleeping, he took one of the man's ribs and closed up the place with flesh. Then the LORD God made a woman from the rib he had taken out of the man, and he brought her to the man.

There are more problems as we go on. Why was Cain afraid of being killed (4:14)? Who would there be to kill him? And from where did he get his wife? The obvious (literal?) reading of 4:14 seems to show that there were a lot of other humans around: 'I will be a restless wanderer on the earth, and whoever finds me will kill me.'

We cannot rule out a literal understanding of these passages, but it does seem reasonable to at least consider whether they are meant to be taken figuratively. This has nothing to do with the findings of modern science. Early in the second century AD, Origen felt drawn to a figurative interpretation of Genesis 2 and 3:

> Who could be found so silly as to believe that God, after the manner of a farmer 'planted trees in a paradise eastward in Eden' ... And when God is said to 'walk in the paradise in the evening ...' I do not think anyone will doubt that these are figurative expressions which indicate certain mysteries through a semblance of history (*First Principles*, 4.3).

The literary-cultural approach

Starting with these clues, the literary-cultural approach looks for other evidence that Genesis 2 and 3 might be intended more as a figurative account than as a simple historical one. There is quite a lot of such evidence. To begin with, the content of Genesis 2 – 3 is structured in a symmetrical way similar to that of Genesis 1, though it is not so obvious (see Figure 4, below).

The story contains a number of word-plays. For instance the word used for pain in 3:16 is not the usual Hebrew one for the pain of childbirth. It seems to have been chosen because it sounds like the Hebrew word for 'tree' (a bit like 'trauma' and 'tree' in English). Similarly, the Hebrew words for 'naked', 'crafty' and 'curse' sound very alike.

In the book of Revelation the serpent (12:15) and the tree of life (22:2) are clearly used in a symbolic, non-literal

2:4–6 Introduction

2:7–17 Adam created and placed in Eden.	3:20–24 Adam and Eve driven out of Eden.
2:18–25 Relationships established between mankind and the animals, and man and woman.	3:14–19 The effect on the relationships between man and woman, and mankind and nature.
3:1–5 The serpent's question.	3:8–13 God's question.

3:6–7 Eve and Adam eat the forbidden fruit.

Figure 4 *The structure of Genesis 2 and 3*

133

way. Might that be the case in Genesis, too? It is also pointed out that, in the literature of the Ancient Near East, paradise, the serpent and the tree of life are common religious symbols.

To say that Genesis 2 and 3 give a figurative, symbolic account is not to say that it is unhistorical. Real historical events can be described in a symbolic way. To describe something symbolically can actually be a powerful way of bringing out its significance. Revelation 12:1–6 describes forcefully – and symbolically – how the Messiah came from the people of God in the face of Satan's opposition.

The elements in the story of Revelation 12 are readily accepted as symbolic by most readers because they are so 'extraordinary' in nature. Added to this there is the fact that they are drawn from imagery found in the Old Testament and in Greco-Roman literature. The story in Genesis 2 and 3 may seem less obviously symbolic. However, it contains 'extraordinary' elements (a pile of clay becomes a man, a talking serpent, a tree of life) and these images are found in other Ancient Near Eastern literature. So, it is reasonable to take seriously the possibility that this is a symbolic narrative.

When a historical event is described in a non-literal, symbolic way, we cannot get behind the symbolic language to reconstruct a simple historical account of the events to which it refers unless we have other evidence to help us. If Revelation 12:1–6 were the only account we had of Christ's coming, we could not reconstruct the historical event. But, in fact, we do have the accounts in the Gospels which give us the historical details. Genesis 2 – 3 does seem to refer to a definite historical event because of the geographical setting given to it, the genealogies which follow it and which give it a chronological setting, and the use made of the story in the New Testament, especially in Romans 5. However, if it is written in symbolic language we have to be very cautious in what we try to say about this event. Even so, as we shall see, it is possible to make some suggestions about it with the help of other evidence. As a result, the literary-cultural approach makes good sense of Genesis 2 – 3. Since it also takes seriously the clearly symbolic language of the story, it seems more satisfactory than the literal approach.

The first people

Who was Adam?

One possible reconstruction of the historical background to Genesis 2 and 3 has been suggested in a book entitled *Who Was Adam?* by a biblical scholar and anthropologist, Canon E. K. V. Pearce.

Pearce starts with the picture the Bible gives us of Adam and his family's way of life both before and after they left Eden. They are shown tilling the soil and herding animals. There is the implication that they used stone tools, since one of their descendants, Tubal-Cain, seems to have been the first person to use metal: '... Tubal-Cain, who forged all kinds of tools out of bronze and iron' (Genesis 4:22). In scientific terms, Adam's way of life would be described as 'Neolithic' or New Stone Age. In the Old Stone Age food was obtained by hunting and by gathering wild plants, not by farming. The Bronze Age followed the Neolithic Age.

Pearce points out that the Neolithic culture arose in the uplands of Turkey which, as we saw, is one possible site for Eden. From there it spread to Europe, Asia and the Middle East. The beginning of the Neolithic Age is usually dated around 8000 BC. Interestingly, Cain is said to have built a city (4:17), and archaeologists have found

Neolithic cities. One of the earliest is Catal Huyuk in upland Turkey.

Pearce's suggestion has been taken up by quite a number of evangelical scholars who accept that there is good evidence for an 'old earth' and that creatures looking like modern humans (*Homo sapiens sapiens*) have existed on earth for at least 50,000 years. (See most recently M. A. Jeeves and R. J. Berry, *Science, Life and Christian Belief* [Leicester: IVP, 1998], p. 111f.; M. L. Lubenow in *Bones of Contention* [pp. 234–241] critiques Pearce's suggestion as one of the two major evangelical 'old earth' views of human origins.) The suggestion is irrelevant for 'young earth' creationists, since for them the evidence of Neolithic culture has to be dated to after the global flood, and so cannot be related to Adam and Eve. However, this leaves the quite striking correspondences between the culture depicted in Genesis 2 – 4 and Neolithic culture as mere coincidence. Moreover, the existence of an Old Stone Age culture prior to the Neolithic after the flood is odd, since Genesis 9:20 depicts Noah as a cultivator of the soil like Adam and Cain.

Pearce's view is no more than a plausible suggestion. It leaves unanswered the questions of exactly what happened in Eden, and of how Adam and his descendants are to be related to the fossil creatures that are supposed to be the ancestors of modern human beings. We must now consider what can be said about this, always remembering that a good deal of guesswork is involved. As we do this, we will see some of the problems associated with acceptance of a Neolithic Adam and Eve.

Who was Cain's wife?

Those who reject the theory of evolution, whether on the basis of a literal interpretation of Genesis 1 – 2 or some other grounds, regard the creation of Adam and Eve as a special act of God. They see some of the so-called 'fossil men' as ape-like creatures which were in no way human, and others as fully human, so that there are no transitional forms. Cain's wife, then, has to be one of his sisters, and his fear expressed in 4:14 was a fear of future relatives of his, not yet born.

Christians who accept evolution argue that God used that process to bring into being a physical body appropriate for the spiritual nature made in God's image – human nature. They point out that the image of God referred to in Genesis 1:27 cannot be our physical appearance: 'So God created man in his own image, in the image of God he created him; male and female he created them.' God is spirit and does not have a physical body. Genesis 2:7 is taken as saying in picture language that we are made partly of dust, just like the animals, but also have a spiritual nature which survives our physical death and the return of our body to the dust: 'the LORD God formed the man from the dust of the ground and breathed into his nostrils the breath of life, and the man became a living being.' It is this spiritual nature which makes us human beings and not just animals. Since we do not really understand the relationship between the physical and non-physical aspects of our being (the body-mind and body-soul relationships have been much debated by philosophers and theologians down through the centuries), we cannot say how God brought the two into union. The moment he did this, the first humans were created.

Those who accept Pearce's suggestion differ over

whether the change that resulted in Adam and Eve being creatures made in the image of God was the result of a special act of God, or whether it was the culmination of a process guided by God.

The fossil evidence is of little relevance in the debate about when the first humans (as defined in biblical terms – creatures bearing God's image) appeared. Fossils, by their nature, can be classified only on the basis of their physical features – whether the creature walked upright, its brain size and so on. There is no reason why possession of the image of God, a spiritual quality, should be related to any change in physical form.

Anthropologists try to classify the fossil creatures using the evidence of how they lived; for instance, the use of tools. However, some animals make use of sticks and stones as primitive tools, and so this is not a sure test of humanness. Some early paintings and figurines have been taken as evidence of a 'religious sense', but this is pure speculation. Even evidence of deliberate burial of the dead with some ritual acts does not prove the existence of a God-consciousness. It might only express a sense of love and respect for the one now dead. In fact, the earliest clear evidence of creatures worshipping God seems to be the existence of religious sanctuaries, found in the Neolithic city of Catal Huyuk.

Whatever else may be in dispute, biologists and anthropologists agree that all the existing races of human beings belong to one single, unified species, which they call *Homo sapiens sapiens*. They believe that this species originated at least 50,000 years ago.

Christian evolutionists who date Adam and Eve to the Neolithic era have to accept that when they received the image of God – human nature – there would have been many other creatures just like them physically. These too would have been able to receive human nature. Maybe, they suggest, after the fall God conferred (fallen) human nature on all those who shared Adam and Eve's physical nature. The existence of these other beings would explain both Cain's fear and where his wife came from. Does this idea, however, fit with other biblical statements about human origins?

On examination, none of the key biblical passages clearly rules out this idea. Romans 5:12–21 stresses a single sinful act as the source of human sinfulness but does not say how sin spread to all humans from that act. Indeed, it is argued, in this passage Jesus is linked spiritually, not physically, to those who receive life through his obedience. The same could be true of those who receive death through Adam's sin. 1 Corinthians 15:45–48 calls Adam 'the first man' and says that all subsequent humans share his nature, but there is nothing in the evolutionists' view to contradict this since nothing is said of how this nature was passed on. Paul's statement in Acts 17:26 that 'From one man [God] made every nation of men' could mean this, but since Adam is not mentioned in the Greek text (the Greek just says 'one', not even 'one man') it could simply be a general way of stressing the unity of the human race. Finally, there is Genesis 3:20, where we are told that Adam named his wife Eve 'because she was the mother of all the living'. This is often assumed to say that she is the physical ancestor of all humans. However, Christian evolutionists argue that that is not what it actually says. It speaks of 'all the living'. This is significant, coming just after the sin which has led to the sentence of death on the human race and the hint of salvation through the seed of the woman. 'The living' here may then refer to those who will find life through the coming saviour. These interpretations of Acts 17:26 and

Can we believe Genesis today?

Genesis 3:20 are debatable but not impossible.

This discussion of the biblical evidence seems to indicate that acceptance of evolution as the process that God used to bring human beings into existence does not lead to any necessary conflict with the Bible. If that is the case, we are left to decide whether or not to accept the theory of evolution on the basis of the scientific evidence.

The 'African Eve' hypothesis

During the 1990s there has been quite a lot of discussion among scientists about the so-called 'Mitochondrial Eve' or 'African Eve' hypothesis. This has been picked up in the popular media. Mitochondria are important sub-units in the living cells which make up our body. They act as the 'powerhouse' of the cell. They contain within them a form of the hereditary material DNA. A significant feature of this mitochondrial DNA is that, in both men and women, it is derived only from the mother. Changes (mutations) can occur in the DNA during the copying process that goes on when new mitochondria are formed. As a result, the longer that particular human populations are isolated from one another, the greater are the differences between their mitochondrial DNA. By studying the degrees of difference between the mitochondrial DNA of present-day geographically separated populations, scientists have been able to draw up a 'family tree' of the mother's line of descent of modern humans. This suggests that all present-day humans have a common origin in Africa. By estimating the rate of mutation, the common mother – the 'African Eve' – can be dated, very approximately, to about 200,000 years ago. Although it seems to be gaining in acceptance, this hypothesis is still quite controversial among genetic scientists and biologists interested in human evolution. It seems premature and unwise at this stage of the debate to attempt to relate this to biblical ideas.

Studies of the genetic diversity of the hereditary unit called the Y-chromosome, which only men have, suggest a common male ancestor for all modern human males. The date of this 'Genetic Adam' is also, very approximately, 200,000 years ago. The similarity in the date with that for the 'Mitochondrial Eve' should not be pressed, as both dates are very approximate.

Note on radiocarbon dating

The dating of the most recent fossils, including those that are supposed to be human, is done using a radioactive form of carbon called carbon–14 (C–14). This method can only be applied to the remains of living things, and so it cannot be used to date rocks. In addition, the relatively rapid rate at which C–14 breaks down means that it cannot be used to date things more than about 40,000 years old. For this reason, radiocarbon dating is not relevant when discussing the age of the earth. Its major importance lies in its use for dating supposedly human fossils. The reliability of this dating technique has been especially strongly attacked by the 'young earth, flood geology' school of creationists.

It is certainly the most inaccurate of the radioactive dating techniques. The reason for this is well known. Living creatures absorb C–14 from the air while alive. When they die, this stops and the amount of C–14 in their remains decays according to the normal law of radioactive decay. The problem is that the C–14 in the air is produced by the nitrogen molecules in the air being bombarded by cosmic rays. The intensity of this bombardment varies, and, as a result, so does the concentration of C–14. This makes it difficult to be sure exactly how much C–14 there was in a fossil when the creature that produced it died. There are ways around this difficulty, but it is a major reason for the inaccuracy in this dating method. Another problem is that the original determination of the rate at which C–14 breaks down was slightly wrong (by about 3%), and so the initial dates determined by this method have had to be corrected.

It is possible to cross-check C–14 dates back to about 5000 BC by counting the tree rings of some very old, slow-growing trees, such as the bristlecone pines of North America. These cross-checks show that the dates are reasonably reliable and certainly by no means as wildly inaccurate as some critics claim.

The fall and its effects

This brings us to the matter of the disobedience of Adam and Eve (usually referred to as 'the fall') and its effects on creation.

The fall, sin and death

Many Christians think that all death, human and non-human, is a result of the fall. This raises a practical problem. How would the earth support an ever-growing population of creatures if there were no death (think of the rabbit population alone!)?

In addition, the assumption that death for all creatures resulted from the fall is, I believe, based on a misreading of the Bible. The discovery of fossils led to the question of death and the fall being discussed in the nineteenth century long before the theory of evolution came on the scene. Dr J. Orr, a noted Scottish evangelical theologian

and, like G. F. Wright one of the original 'funda-
mentalists', summed up the result of a century of debate
when he wrote,

> There is not a word in the Bible to indicate that
> in its view death entered the animal world as a
> consequence of the sin of man (*The Christian View
> of God and the World* [Edinburgh: Andrew Elliot,
> 1904], p 197).

On the contrary, it would seem that the Bible speaks of
death as a penalty for sin only in relation to men and
women.

It is also important to think about what the Bible
means by death. God said to Adam that he was not to eat
the fruit of the tree of the knowledge of good and evil
because 'when [literally, on the day that] you eat of it you
will surely die' (Genesis 2:17). But they did not die
immediately. Adam lived to be 930! Was God bluffing, as
the serpent suggested (3:4)? No. The answer lies in the
difference between the biblical view of death and ours. We
tend to think of it in purely physical terms, as the moment
when our physical existence ends. However, the various
biblical references to death make most sense when death is
seen as a spiritual power, not just an event at the end of
life. It is a power which weakens and diminishes life,
eventually leading to its end. One falls into the power of
death when cut off from God, the source of life (see
Deuteronomy 30:15–20). This non-physical meaning of
death is clearly meant in John 8:51: 'I tell you the truth, if
anyone keeps my word, he will never see death.' In this
sense Adam and Eve began to experience death as soon as
they were expelled from Eden, where they had lived in
close communion with God.

What is said of the tree of life in Genesis 2 and 3, especially in 3:22, implies that Adam and Eve were not naturally immortal: 'And the LORD God said, "The man has now become like one of us, knowing good and evil. He must not be allowed to reach out his hand and take also from the tree of life and eat, and live for ever."' What their physical destiny would have been if they had not sinned we cannot say. Some have suggested that their life on this earth would have ended the way Enoch's seems to have, being taken into the presence of God without dying physically (Genesis 5:24). Others argue that it is only spiritual death (separation from God) which was the result of the fall. Against this it is argued that in the New Testament the victory of Jesus as Saviour includes victory over physical death (1 Corinthians 15:53–57), implying that for the descendants of Adam it is a consequence of sin.

This discussion indicates that the death which results from sin is not to be equated simply with physical death, and that the Bible presents it as a penalty due to humans alone. There is nothing in the Bible to say that the death of animals is in itself an evil, or that it did not happen before the fall, or that it would not have happened had there been no fall. This also applies to those human-like creatures which existed before God brought into being creatures made in the image of God – true humans in biblical terms. Also, there is no reason to attribute moral value to the purely physical process of degeneration which leads to animal death. As we have seen earlier, moral values only come into play when dealing with moral beings, humans.

Nature and the fall

[14]So the LORD God said to the serpent, 'Because you have done this,

> 'Cursed are you above all the livestock
>> and all the wild animals!
> You will crawl on your belly
>> and you will eat dust
>> all the days of your life.
> [15]And I will put enmity
>> between you and the woman,
>> and between your offspring and hers;
> he will crush your head,
>> and you will strike his heel.'

[16]To the woman he said,

> 'I will greatly increase your pains in child-
>>> bearing;
>> with pain you will give birth to children.
> Your desire will be for your husband,
>> and he will rule over you.'

[17]To Adam he said, 'Because you listened to your wife and ate from the tree about which I commanded you, "You must not eat of it,"

> 'Cursed is the ground because of you;
>> through painful toil you will eat of it
>> all the days of your life.
> [18]It will produce thorns and thistles for you,
>> and you will eat the plants of the field.
> [19]By the sweat of your brow
>> you will eat your food
>> until you return to the ground,

> since from it you were taken;
> for dust you are
> and to dust you will return.'
>
> (Genesis 3:14–19)

What, apart from the death for humans, has been the effect of the fall? The simple answer to this is that we do not really know. Paul in Romans 8:18–23 says that the entry of sin into the world has had an effect that is not restricted to human death. However, the verses in Genesis 3:14–19 are not very detailed. In addition, we are told so little about life in Eden before the fall that if we try to say much about the wider effects of the fall we end up in unfounded and fruitless speculation.

One point worth stressing is that the emphasis in these verses is not on changes in *things* (with the exception of the serpent, which is a symbol of all that is opposed to God), but on changes in *relationships*. The relationship between human beings and their Creator is ruptured. As a result of this, a person's relationship with himself or herself is damaged (there is guilt and shame). People can no longer get on together in harmony (Adam blames Eve). The previously harmonious relationship between humans and the rest of creation is lost.

We cannot say what kind of changes, if any, this made to non-human nature. The statement about 'thorns and thistles' in 3:18 need not mean that they had not existed before, but only that our ability to cultivate the plants we want has been impaired by the fall and the loss of a proper *rapport* with nature. It is sometimes assumed that such things as earthquakes and storms are a result of the fall. But this would require a major change in the laws of nature (which, of course, God is free to change) and seems contrary to the evidence of geology. Maybe the result of

146

the fall is not that these things happen, but that we lack the power which Jesus, the perfect human being, had to deal with nature.

Evolution and the fall

It is sometimes said, both by evolutionists and their opponents, that evolution means humans have gradually become better morally. But this commits the logical mistake which we discussed in chapter 1 of trying to make statements of moral value on a scientific basis.

As a biological theory, as distinct from a philosophical position, evolution says no more or less than that *Homo sapiens sapiens* has become gradually more complex in certain ways and better adapted physically to life on earth. This says nothing about our moral progress or decline. Indeed, as we have seen, science cannot say anything about the origin or basis of morality. Some have tried to find a basis for it in natural instincts. The problem, as always, is that it is necessary to go outside of science to evaluate these. For example, some 'evolutionary moralists' emphasize aggression, others emphasize co-operativeness. Both groups can make a case for these being essential for survival in an evolutionary framework! The truth is that both these traits can be used for good or for evil. Aggression can be directed to fight against what is evil. People can co-operate with one another against God, as we shall see in Genesis 11.

The genealogies

Before leaving Genesis 2 – 5 we need to say something about the genealogies in chapters 4 – 5 and elsewhere in Genesis 1 – 11. We have seen that literalists are happy to accept that these may be selective and incomplete and that, if so, there is no problem about dating Adam to 8000 or 10,000 BC. But should we take the numbers literally?

All the ages given in the standard Hebrew Bible (there are differences in the Samaritan and Greek versions) are multiples of five, with either seven or fourteen added occasionally (e.g. Adam lived for 930 years = 186 x 5; Seth lived for 912 years = (181 x 5) + 7). This could hardly be accidental, and may indicate that the numbers are symbolic in some way which we fail to understand.

It is worth comparing the genealogies in Genesis with others from the Ancient Near East to see if we can learn something about how genealogies were used in the culture from which the Old Testament comes. There is a striking parallel to Genesis in what are called 'king lists' from ancient Sumeria, a culture which existed in southern Babylonia from about 3000 to 2300 BC. These lists date from well before the time of Abraham. The parallels between them and Genesis are set out below.

Sumerian king lists:	*Genesis:*
The creation of kingship	The creation of people
8 or 10 kings, each ruling between 43,000 and 18,600 years	10 patriarchs, each living between 969 and 365 years
The flood	The flood
More kings, each ruling between 1500 and 100 years	More patriarchs, each living between 600 and 110 years

The overall pattern is the same, though the biblical numbers are smaller than the Sumerian ones. To add to the parallels, in Sumerian tradition the seventh king was taken to heaven to have the secrets of the gods revealed to him. Compare this with Enoch, the seventh patriarch.

We shall return to this list when discussing the flood, but the relevant point for us at the moment is that one of the later kings in the Sumerian list, En-Mebaragisi, is said to have reigned for 900 years. He is known from other evidence to have been a real person who lived for a quite normal time. Clearly the numbers here do not seem intended to be taken literally. Perhaps our problem is that 300 years of modern science have given us expectations regarding the use of numbers that are wrong when dealing with their use by the peoples of the Ancient Near East. Unfortunately, we do not have any definite clues to help us understand the symbolic meaning of these large numbers in either the Sumerian or the biblical lists. Presumably the decrease in the lengths of reigns and lives symbolizes a decline of some kind in the human race. In Genesis this is, no doubt, primarily a moral decline.

Further reading

R. J. Berry, *God and Evolution* (London: Hodder & Stoughton, 1988). Advocates a theistic evolution position.

R. Dawkins, *River Out of Eden* (London: Phoenix, 1995). Contains a chapter which gives details of the 'African Eve' hypothesis.

R. Leakey, *The Origins of Humankind* (London: Phoenix, 1995). A fairly brief, readable presentation of the secular evolutionary view of human origins.

M. L. Lubenow, *Bones of Contention* (Grand Rapids, MI; Baker, 1992). A 'young earth' creationist assessment of human fossils.

E. K. V. Pearce, *Who Was Adam?* (Exeter: Paternoster, 1969). Argues for a Neolithic dating of Adam and Eve.

8

Events in Genesis 6 – 11

The story of Noah's flood is one of the best-known Bible stories. As we shall see, there is no doubt that it was a historical catastrophe. The Bible makes it clear that the flood was an act of God's judgment on the human race because of its wickedness. Genesis 6:1–4 gives one example of that wickedness. Unfortunately, the passage in which that comes is a very puzzling one:

> ¹When men began to increase in number on the earth and daughters were born to them, ²the sons of God saw that the daughters of men were beautiful, and they married any of them they chose. ³Then the LORD said, 'My Spirit will not contend with man for ever, for he is mortal; his days will be a hundred and twenty years.'
>
> ⁴The Nephilim were on the earth in those days – and also afterwards – when the sons of God went to the daughters of men and had children by them.

They were the heroes of old, men of renown.

[5]The LORD saw how great man's wickedness on the earth had become, and that every inclination of the thoughts of his heart was only evil all the time. [6]The LORD was grieved that he had made man on the earth, and his heart was filled with pain. [7]So the LORD said, 'I will wipe mankind, whom I have created, from the face of the earth – men and animals, and creatures that move along the ground, and birds of the air – for I am grieved that I have made them.' [8]But Noah found favour in the eyes of the LORD (Genesis 6:1–8).

The sons of God

Who were these 'sons of God' who entered into marriages with the 'daughters of men' and so displeased God? At least three interpretations have received some support.

Fallen angels

Many take them to be fallen angels. The main support for this is that the usual meaning for the phrase 'sons of God' in the Old Testament is 'heavenly beings' (e.g. Job 1:6; Psalm 29:1). One objection to this interpretation is that it seems unfair of God to punish humans for an act instigated by fallen angels. A possible reply is that both the women concerned and their fathers consented to these irregular unions, knowing that they were wrong.

Descendants of Seth

An almost equally popular view takes 'the sons of God' to be a reference to Seth's descendants. The list of Seth's descendants in Genesis 5 makes no mention of any sinful acts committed by them and includes the two exceptionally godly men, Enoch and Noah. Genesis 4:17–24 gives Cain's line. This includes Lamech, who committed bigamy and two vengeful murders. So, it is argued, the Sethites were more godly than the Cainites, and therefore their marriages with Cainite women displeased God. The unusual use of the phrase 'the sons of God' which this requires is a major objection to this view. It may be justified by the fact that in Exodus 4:22, and elsewhere, Israel is called God's 'son', and the Israelites are ultimately descended from Seth.

Ritual prostitution

A third, more recent and less well-known interpretation sees as the background to the story the practice of ritual prostitution that was connected with many of the fertility cults of the Ancient Near East. In this case, 'the sons of God' could refer to the priests or kings who were supposed to represent the pagan god in the sexual rites practised in the worship of the fertility gods. This is a plausible interpretation but, with such an unclear passage, one cannot be certain that it is right.

The difficult passage in 1 Peter 3:18–20, which refers to the disobedience before the flood, can be interpreted to support any of these views.

Because none of the arguments for or against the different interpretations seems conclusive, it would be wrong to insist that any one of them is *the* right one. All we can do is say which one seems to be the most likely.

The second interpretation seems the least likely. This is because it requires the unusual meaning of 'Sethite' for 'the sons of God' and because it is not at all clear from

Genesis 4 – 5 that we are meant to see the Sethites as a whole as markedly more godly than the Cainites. The first interpretation has the merit of taking 'sons of God' in its most common Old Testament sense. However, since Genesis 1 – 11 is full of implicit attacks on the pagan religious practices and ideas of the Ancient Near East, I find the third interpretation the most likely.

The Nephilim

The Nephilim of 6:4 are mentioned only once elsewhere in the Bible, in Numbers 13:33. There the Israelite spies meet them in Canaan and describe them as being of 'great size'. Some take the Nephilim to be the children of the irregular marriages. However, Genesis 6:4 does not actually say that, but only that they existed at the time such marriages happened. This can be taken to imply that they existed before there were any such children. If they were the children of the marriages which displeased God, it is surprising that they survived the flood, which was partly a punishment for these marriages.

Words can change their meaning or have more than one meaning. The fact that the word 'Nephilim' only occurs twice, in stories relating to very different periods of time, means that we cannot be sure that it has the same meaning in both places. In either place it *could* refer to a distinct race of people but there is no fossil evidence of a distinct group of very tall people having existed in the Near East at any time. This does not, however, mean that such a group did not exist, since the fossil evidence is very limited. Quite apart from this, it seems probable that 'Nephilim' was a term for people who were outstanding in some way, without implying that they were a special race on their own. In Numbers 13:33 the outstanding feature is size. The 'renown' in Genesis 6:4 probably refers to their quality as warriors, since that is a common meaning of the word which the NIV translates as 'heroes' in this verse.

The flood

Stories of a great flood are known from cultures around the world. J. G. Frazer quotes about 140 in his book *Folklore in the Old Testament*. We need to take care, though, in the significance we attach to this. There is reason to believe that some of the stories that have been collected are in fact retellings of the biblical story, first heard from missionaries. Secondly, many of them are widely different in detail from the biblical story and could have their origin in some quite different flood experience. After all, major floods do occur in many places from time to time. We will look at two aspects of the flood – its historicity and its universality – and at some of the practical details that are mentioned in the Genesis account.

A historical flood?

There is one set of flood stories so similar to the biblical one that it is generally agreed that they originated in the same historical event. These are the flood stories from Mesopotamia. The best preserved of them is part of a long Babylonian poem called *The Gilgamesh Epic*. An earlier version of the story is found in another poem from Babylonia called *The Atrahasis Epic*. Both of these are known to have existed by about 1600 BC. A much earlier and fragmentary Sumerian account of the flood has also survived. In both *The Atrahasis Epic* and the Sumerian account there is an account of the creation of human beings followed by various divine judgments, culminating in the flood. This parallels the pattern of events in Genesis 1 – 9.

The main similarities between the Mesopotamian and biblical stories are these:

- After the multiplication of mankind a divine decision is taken to send a punishing flood to destroy them.
- One man is told to save himself, his family and some animals, by building a boat.
- A great flood destroys the rest of mankind.
- The boat grounds on a mountain in southern Armenia.
- Three times birds are sent out to determine when the land is habitable.
- The hero offers a sacrifice and is given a divine blessing.

There are also many differences between the Mesopotamian and biblical stories. The most obvious is that the Mesopotamian one assumes the existence of many gods, with Enlil as the chief god. More detailed differences are:

- Enlil wants to destroy mankind because their noisiness disturbs him, not because of their sinfulness.
- Contrary to the will of Enlil and the other gods, a god called Enki warns one of his devoted worshippers to build a boat to escape the coming flood.
- The hero does not warn other people, but hides the reason for his boat-building from them.
- The size and shape of the boat, the passengers, and the duration of the flood all differ from the biblical story.
- The birds sent out are a dove, a swallow, and a raven.
- The divine blessing is immortality for the hero and his wife.

Most of these differences have to do with the

understanding of the significance of the flood and we will look at them in the next chapter. Other differences might have arisen as a result of changes as the story was constantly retold. It is unlikely that the biblical story is based directly on one of the existing Mesopotamian versions, or vice versa. Most likely, both they and the biblical story share a common source.

We saw in the last chapter that the Sumerian king lists also mention the flood as a major disruption in history. Unfortunately, the strange use of numbers in those lists means that they give no help in dating the flood. Since Sumerian history is fairly well documented by inscriptions from 2600 BC onwards with no mention of the flood, it must have happened earlier than this, probably a good deal earlier.

A universal flood?

There is no doubt that until about a century ago nearly everyone took the story of the flood to refer to a universal flood covering the whole earth. It was primarily the impact of scientific considerations which led people to think again and to re-examine the biblical account, to see whether it really did have to be understood in this way. If we take the flood as being universal, we need to think about three difficulties raised by scientific studies.

Firstly, there does not appear to be any evidence for a world-wide flood. In order for the Himalayas to be covered, the water would need to have been nearly six miles or nine kilometres deep. We would expect such a flood to have left thick layers of sediment that geologists could not miss. They have not, however, found them.

Advocates of the 'flood geology' school, have, as we have seen, proposed that it is all, or most of, the fossil-bearing rocks, and many others, that are the result of the flood. Most geologists, however, think that there are many rock formations, some bearing fossils, which just cannot be explained by 'flood geology'. This is a rather technical subject, and those who want to follow it up should read the books by D. A. Young (who holds to an anti-evolutionary, age-day position) listed in this book (see pp. 90, 106 and 168). They are written in fairly popular terms.

Some creationists (e.g. Morris and Parker, *What is Creation Science?*, pp. 195f., 219) refer to the so-called 'fossil graveyards' as evidence of a cataclysmic, world-wide flood. However, this interpretation faces a major problem. The Karroo formation in Africa contains the remains of perhaps 800 billion vertebrate animals (Morris and Parker's figure). These creatures vary in size from lizards to animals the size of cows. A simple calculation shows that if all these creatures lived at the same time, as the 'flood geology' interpretation requires, and were spread over the whole surface of the earth (assuming none of the earth was covered with seas), they would each have 23 square metres of land (about 200 square feet). However, the Karroo formation is only one of several such 'fossil graveyards'. If it contains only 1% (almost certainly a gross over-estimate) of the total number of creatures in such formations, then each animal alive at the time of the flood would have had less than a quarter of a square metre (about 2 square feet) of standing-room. It seems far more reasonable to explain these 'fossil-graveyards' as the result of the accumulation of the carcasses of dead animals in a particular place (perhaps by a series of flash floods) over a long period of time.

The second question that must be addressed is: Where did all the water for the flood come from? It would seem that, to cover the whole earth to the depth required, eight times as much water would be needed as there is now in all the oceans.

One explanation is that God could have created this water miraculously and removed it miraculously.

An alternative theory, favoured by some flood geologists, is that between creation and the flood there was a canopy of water vapour above the earth's atmosphere ('the waters above the expanse' mentioned in Genesis 1:7). At the time of the flood, this collapsed to give torrential rain. But this solution gives rise to another problem. Water vapour, like all gases, may be light but it does weigh something. The amount required to flood the earth would raise the atmospheric pressure (the weight of the atmosphere) from its present fifteen pounds per square inch to nearly 1000 pounds per square inch. Everything now alive on the earth's surface would be squashed flat! It could be that the creatures alive then were able to live under that pressure but, even if that was the case, it is difficult to see how they could have coped with the rapid and great drop in pressure when the canopy collapsed. The effects on them would presumably be similar to that on deep-sea divers who, working at just a few times atmospheric pressure, die if they come up too quickly. The gases dissolved in their blood bubble out of it like the gas from a fizzy drink when it is poured out.

As a final point in connection with the theory of the water canopy, it is worth considering whether the reference in Genesis to 'the waters above the expanse' may refer instead to ordinary rain clouds. Psalm 148:4 uses the same phrase in reference to clouds after the flood.

Thirdly, a literal reading of the flood story raises a further difficulty. Genesis 7:20 says that the mountains were covered by more than 20 feet of water: 'The waters rose and covered the mountains to a depth of more than twenty feet.' Presumably Noah knew this because he knew that the Ark floated with about 20 feet of it under the water. When the Ark ran aground on the seventeenth day of the seventh month (8:4), there would have been 20 feet or so of water covering the place where it rested. The dry land could not be seen until the first day of the tenth month (8:5). If it took two and a half months for about 20 feet of water to drain away, how long would a depth of 6 miles take to drain away?

Attempts to get around this problem by suggesting that the Himalayas only came into being after the flood seem incredible. The seismic and volcanic disturbances that this would cause over a relatively short period of a few thousand years would be earth-shattering. There would be frequent very severe earthquakes and the amount of dust thrown into the atmosphere by volcanoes would cut out sunlight and probably cause prolonged ice ages.

With problems like these it seems worth re-examining our understanding of what the Bible says about the flood.

A local flood?

One point worth thinking about is that we would expect a major, world-wide flood to cause major changes on the surface of the earth. However, the way the location of Eden is described suggests that the reader is expected to recognize the location of this pre-flood site. At least two of the four rivers did not disappear in the flood. Here may be a hint that the flood was not universal. If Genesis 2 – 4 does indeed depict Neolithic culture, then there is also the fact that there is no sign in the fossil record of any major break within the Neolithic period, which one might expect on the 'flood geology' hypothesis, especially since, as noted before, Noah is depicted as a farmer like Adam.

Can we believe Genesis today?

'Land' or 'earth'?

Supporters of the idea that the flood was a local catastrophe, not a universal one, argue that the language of the story has been misread. The Hebrew word translated 'earth' in the story (*'ereṣ*) does not mean the same thing as the English word. In three quarters of its occurrences in the Old Testament, it is better translated by the word 'land', meaning a particular place or area, rather than 'earth'. The context has to be the guide. Also, there is a special Hebrew word for the whole inhabitable earth (*tēḇēl*), and it is not used in the flood story. Try reading Genesis 6 – 9 with the word 'land' replacing 'earth' and you will see the different impression you get (usually, where the English has 'earth', the Hebrew has 'the earth/land').

All people or all known people?

Statements like 'I am going to put an end to all people' (6:13) might seem to demand a universal interpretation of the flood. However, it is a feature of Old Testament language to use such apparently all-embracing phrases when they are not meant literally. For example, 'all the countries' in Genesis 41:57 could hardly include the Americas or China, nor can the claim in 1 Kings 18:10 that Ahab searched all the nations and kingdoms for Elijah be taken literally. Hebrew speech is full of such 'exaggeration to make a point', which is not intended to be taken literally. It is quite possible that the flood story uses such language throughout to stress the greatness of the catastrophe but without meaning it literally. At most, it may mean that all the land and people known to Noah were inundated by the flood.

These arguments from the text of the Bible itself do no more than suggest that a local interpretation of the story is possible. Those who adopt such an interpretation do so because they are persuaded that the scientific arguments favour a local flood rather than a universal one.

The location of the flood area

If the flood was only local, where did it happen? Most of those who adopt the local view assume that it occurred in Mesopotamia. This is partly because the story is followed by events in Babylonia, in southern Mesopotamia (the Tower of Babel and Abraham's call). The main reason, though, is the existence of the Mesopotamian flood stories. These are clearly set in Babylonia.

However, it has also been pointed out that the natural reading of the Hebrew of Genesis 11:2 is that the survivors of the flood entered Babylonia *from the east*: 'As men moved from the east, they found a plain in Shinar [Babylonia] and settled there' (translation incorporating the NIV footnote). It is then suggested that the flood occurred in the upland plateaux to the north and east of Babylonia, near the possible site of the garden of Eden and the mountains of Ararat. There is evidence that the Sumerians migrated to southern Babylonia from elsewhere, probably from further north. They may have brought the flood story with them and gradually adapted its details to match their new homeland.

In view of the lack of geographical evidence in the biblical story, other than the mention of the mountains of Ararat to the north-east of Mesopotamia, all attempts to define the location of a local flood must be speculative.

Even if the flood was local, it could still have destroyed all humans other than those in the Ark if, at that time, they still lived in a restricted area. This view is hard to evaluate since we cannot say much about the possible date of the flood. However, if we link Adam with Neolithic culture, that culture did spread out from eastern Turkey quite rapidly. This means that a flood to wipe out all human beings would need to have happened fairly soon after the fall – a matter of a few hundred years later rather than thousands of years later.

From a purely numerical point of view, there is nothing absurd in the suggestion that the present population of the earth might all be descended from eight people (Noah, his wife, his three sons and their wives) who lived about 5000–3000 BC. This would require the population to double every 150 to 200 years. And, between 1630 and 1930, it has been estimated that the earth's population did indeed double every 130 years.

The animals in the Ark

[19]You are to bring into the ark two of all living creatures, male and female, to keep them alive with you. [20]Two of every kind of bird, of every kind of animal and of every kind of creature that moves along the ground will come to you to be kept alive. [21]You are to take every kind of food that is to be eaten and store it away as food for you and for them (Genesis 6:19–21).

These verses raise a number of questions which are difficult to answer if the flood was universal. It is not a matter of what God *could* do, but what seems consistent with the way the story is told in Genesis, in which there is no indication of God doing a series of miracles to bring the animals to Noah, keep them alive on the Ark for just over a year and then disperse them all over the earth. For instance, how did the animals get from distant lands to the Ark? Unless the whole face of the earth was very different from what it is now, many would face insurmountable barriers such as major rivers, mountain ranges and oceans. Some, like sloths and tortoises, would take a very long time to get to the Ark! How did they migrate home afterwards, when the earth was much as it is now? Once they were in the Ark, the problems of feeding and caring for them would be enormous. Could just eight people feed, clean and generally look after tens, even hundreds, of thousands of creatures? Many more people are needed to run a large zoo today, which has far fewer animals! Very different living conditions would be needed by the various animals: some would need to be kept very cold, while others would need it to be hot. Some would need to live in arid desert conditions, while others would need to be cool and moist. How could this have been managed?

By miraculous intervention, God could, of course, ensure that all these problems were solved – but the story gives no hint of God doing so.

These problems do not arise, however, if the flood was only local; the number of animals involved would be very much fewer and the range of their needs less demanding. The language of the story would allow this, given what we have already seen of the tendency of Hebrew speech to 'exaggerate to make a point'.

A local or a universal flood? We have seen that the biblical account can be understood as referring to a local flood. There is no indisputable geological evidence for a universal flood, and there are some strong scientific arguments against it. This leads me to the conclusion that the flood was a local catastrophe that occurred somewhere in the Near East. The Sumerians knew of it, but it does not form part of the written records from Sumeria, which go back to about 3000 BC. This would indicate that the flood happened some time earlier than that.

The Tower of Babel

[1]Now the whole world had one language and a common speech. [2]As men moved eastward, they found a plain in Shinar and settled there.

[3]They said to each other, 'Come, let's make bricks and bake them thoroughly.' They used brick instead of stone, and bitumen for mortar. [4]Then they said, 'Come let us build ourselves a city, with a tower that reaches to the heavens, so that we may make a name for ourselves and not be scattered over the face of the whole earth.'

[5]But the LORD came down to see the city and the tower that the men were building. [6]The LORD said, 'If as one people speaking the same language they have begun to do this, then nothing they plan to do will be impossible for them. [7]Come, let us go down and confuse their language so that they will not understand each other.'

[8]So the LORD scattered them from there over all the earth, and they stopped building the city. [9]That is why it was called Babel – because there the LORD confused the language of the whole world. From there the LORD scattered them over the face of the whole earth (Genesis 11:1–9).

The purpose of the story

For anyone who is acquainted with Babylonian literature and religion, Genesis 11:1–9 reads like a brilliant satire on the foundation of Babylon and its temples. No doubt this was what the author intended. It is interesting, and probably significant, that the Babylonian creation story *Enuma Elish* ends with the building of Babylon and the temple of Marduk, the chief god of Babylon and creator of the heavens and the earth.

In Akkadian, the language of Mesopotamia in Old Testament times, the name of Babylon is Babel. This means 'The Gate of Heaven'. The author of Genesis, however, links the name with the Hebrew verb meaning 'to confuse' (*balal*). The most striking structure in ancient Babylon was a great stepped pyramid, called *Etemenanki*, 'The Temple Foundation of Heaven and Earth.' It was thought of as linking earth to heaven. The chief building in the temple enclosure was the temple of Marduk. This was called *Esagila*, 'The Temple that Raises its Head.' In the creation story its builders are said to have 'raised its head on high'.

The relevance of all this to the understanding of Genesis 11:1–9 is obvious. The writer is making fun of the claims of pagan religions to be the way to God. Instead of being an expression of human worship of God and the link between heaven and earth, the temple tower is an expression of human pride and a form of rebellion against the true God. The 'Gate of Heaven' becomes the source of confusion and disunity among humans.

Historical significance

If this is the religious meaning of the story, what does it tell us historically? The answer to this depends on how the flood is understood. Those who believe that the flood, whether universal or local, destroyed all humans other than Noah's family take this story to mark the beginning of the diversity of human languages and races.

In fact, the story does not necessarily claim this. Some argue that it describes what happened to one group of those who migrated from the area where the Ark came to rest, how they were dispersed and their language confused. It leaves open what happened to other groups. Three strands of evidence can be brought together to support this view.

Firstly, the genealogy in Genesis 10 describes the spread of Noah's descendants over the world known to the Israelites. Only one group of these, the sons of Cush, is linked with Babel and Mesopotamia (10:8–12). The genealogies in Genesis 4 and 5 cover the period from the fall to the flood. It seems reasonable, it is argued, to take the genealogy in Genesis 10 as covering a quite lengthy period between the flood and the Tower of Babel incident.

Secondly, it is also argued that the reference in verse 4 to the builders of the tower wanting to make a name for themselves and avoid being scattered implies that there were other people apart from them around. They wanted to be more famous than these people. Also, they feared that without a defensible city they might be attacked, defeated and scattered.

Thirdly, what about the references in the story to 'the whole earth'? Once again, as in the flood story, this could be translated as 'the whole land', meaning a large but limited area such as Mesopotamia. In historical times – that is, from the time that written records began – there has always been more than one language spoken in Mesopotamia at any one time. Genesis 11:1 can be taken as saying that there was once a time when only one language was spoken in the whole of that area. It is interesting that there is a Sumerian epic, 'Enmerkar and the Lord Aratta', which some scholars think tells of a time when people spoke only one language, which the chief god Enki changed into many languages. However, the text is fragmentary and not easy to understand.

Languages can be grouped into 'families' which have

marked similarities in their vocabulary, grammar, and the way they form words, and so on. For example, most of the languages spoken in Europe, Iran and north India belong to the 'Indo-European family' of languages. Middle-Eastern languages such as Aramaic, Hebrew and Arabic belong to the 'Semitic family'. Individual languages within a 'family' probably developed as groups of people who originally all spoke the same language became separated geographically and developed their own special ways of speaking. The development of the Indo-European languages can be explained in this way. Linguistic experts are divided over whether or not there is evidence to suggest that the different 'families' have developed from an original single language. However, if the story of the Tower of Babel does refer to the founding of the famous city of Babylon, we have to reckon with the fact that there is no evidence that Babylon existed earlier than about 2000 BC. We know that by then several different languages did exist. Of course, the story could refer to a much earlier, unsuccessful, attempt to found a city on the site of Babylon.

The evidence is so inconclusive that it seems best to suspend judgment and accept that, even if we believe in a universal destruction of humans by the flood, we should not insist that the Tower of Babel incident explains the origin of all languages. We should accept that it might refer to the origin of only one 'family' of languages. This 'localized' understanding of the Babel incident has to be adopted by those who believe that the flood destroyed only a part of the human race alive at that time.

Further reading

A. C. Custance, *The Flood: Local or global?* (Grand Rapids,

MI: Zondervan, 1979). Argues for a local flood.

S. Dalley, *Myths from Mesopotamia* (Oxford: Oxford University Press, 1991). Contains modern English translations of the myths about creation and the flood.

J. G. Frazer, *Folklore in the Old Testament* (London: Macmillan, 1919). A classic collection, but needs to be used with care.

A. Hayward, *Creation and Evolution: The facts and fallacies*, rev. ed. (London: Triangle, 1994). Contains a chapter which critiques 'flood geology'.

H. M. Morris and G. E. Parker, *What is Creation Science?* (San Diego, CA: Creation-Life Publishers, 1982). A more recent exposition of the 'young earth, flood geology' position than the book by Whitcomb and Morris listed below.

J. C. Whitcomb and H. M. Morris, *The Genesis Flood* (Grand Rapids, MI: Baker Book House, 1961). The classic statement of the 'young earth, flood geology' position.

D. A. Young, *The Biblical Flood* (Carlisle: Paternoster, 1995). An illuminating study of how Christians down the ages have interpreted the biblical flood story.

D. A. Young, *Creation and the Flood* (Grand Rapids, MI: Baker Book House, 1977). Subtitled 'An alternative to flood geology and theistic evolution.'

9

Get the message?

It is inevitable that, as children of a scientific age, we want to relate what we read in Genesis 1 – 11 to the findings of science. It is tragic, though, if we do this at the expense of listening to what Genesis is trying to teach us. We do not need to resolve all the scientific disputes related to it before we can understand this. If we did, all those who have read the Bible without the benefit of modern scientific knowledge have been at a grave disadvantage! It would be surprising if God allowed that to be true of his Word. Arguably, if we need any additional knowledge in order to understand Genesis, knowing something about the religions and cultures of the Ancient Near East is of more value than knowing something about science. It is easier to see what the author's main points are when they are highlighted by contrast with the beliefs he is opposing.

A detailed study of the message of these chapters would require the writing of another book. What follows will be only an outline sketch of that message. Instead of going through it chapter by chapter, we will look at a number of themes: the nature of God; the nature of the world; the problem of evil; what it means to be human; and God's plan of salvation.

What is God like?

Read against the background of the Babylonian, Canaanite or Egyptian religious literature, especially their creation stories, the striking thing about Genesis 1 – 3 is its monotheism, its assumption that *there is only one God*. One form of the Babylonian creation epic begins with the birth of the gods from the waters of chaos. Marduk, the god of Babylon, gains his superior position by overcoming the forces of chaos and creating the world. In Genesis there is only ever one God, the Creator. The 'us' of 1:26 ('Then God said, "Let us make man in our image, in our likeness"') in no way contradicts this. It may be a royal 'we', or an address to the heavenly court of (non-divine) angels. It may prepare the way for the later trinitarian understanding of God, but it does not proclaim it.

We have seen in chapter 5 that the reference to the sun and moon as merely 'lights' is a rejection of the worship of the heavenly bodies as gods. Marduk of Babylon was the sun-god. If the traditional understanding of 1:1–2 is correct, then we are being told that *God existed alone before anything was created*. There are no primeval, eternal waters of chaos.

Mention of the waters of chaos leads to another aspect of God that is very clear in Genesis 1 in particular – *his sovereign power*. He does not have to do battle with the forces of chaos before creating the world. We have seen that using the special verb 'to create' (*bārā'*) in reference to the creation of the sea monsters (1:21) is an attack on any such idea. God simply speaks and his will is done.

The wisdom of God is displayed in the order and pattern of his work of creation. Proverbs 8:22–31 and Isaiah 40:12–14 take up this theme.

The flood story in Genesis shows *the grace of God*, in striking contrast to the Babylonian story. In the Babylonian story it is only the fact that one of the gods breaks the promise, made by all the gods, not to warn humans of the flood that leads to a few escaping it. In Genesis it is an act of grace on the part of God to warn Noah.

Comparison of the Genesis story with the Babylonian version brings out another aspect of God, *his moral nature*. In Genesis, the flood is clearly an act of judgment on human sinfulness. It is an act of justice, not of selfish pique or revenge. In the Babylonian version, the flood is sent for a quite non-moral reason. Enlil gets irritated and touchy because the humans are so noisy that they disturb his sleep!

So then, Genesis 1 – 11 presents us with the claim that there is one true God, the Creator, who is sovereign over the world. He acts wisely and justly. His justice is seasoned with grace.

What is the world like?

The most obvious thing about the world in Genesis is that it is *a created world*. It owes its existence and character to God and so is dependent on him. This is spelt out more fully in the New Testament (Colossians 1:15–17; Hebrews 1:1–4).

Genesis 1 stresses that, as originally created, *the world was very 'good'*. The meaning of its goodness is clear from the context – it pleased God. It pleased him because it reflected something of himself. One aspect of this was its order and harmony, which is emphasized in the careful structure of the creation account. Such order and harmony is a large part of what is meant by the Hebrew word *šālôm* (*shalom*). This is often translated into English as 'peace', but means not so much the *absence* of conflict or other forms of disturbance as the *presence* of the kind of order and harmony that allows people to live life as God wants it lived. The fact that the creation pleased God also means that it was free of evil, which becomes the major cause of the absence of *shalom* after the fall.

In some religions the material world is thought to be intrinsically evil. Some forms of Greek philosophy taught this, in particular the very influential philosophy of Plato. Basically, all that is 'material' rather than 'spiritual' was seen as 'evil'. The early Christian theologians realized that such a view of the material world is unbiblical. But Greek ideas had such a big impact on western thought that some strands of Christianity are still suspicious of material things and bodily pleasures. These things can, of course, be used in a sinful way, but God's creation is essentially good; it is not wrong to enjoy it as long as we do so in obedience to his law.

Because the world is God's good creation, we should respect it and make use of it responsibly. We are not to despoil and deface it. We shall return to this theme later.

Evil

The goodness of the original creation brings us to the problem of evil. Genesis does not explain the ultimate origin of evil. The serpent is introduced without explanation of how it came to be opposed to God. However, two things are made clear. Firstly, *evil is not something co-equal or co-eternal with God*. The serpent is not another

God but a perverted creature. Secondly, as we have seen, evil is not part of the original nature of creation. Part of God's creation (including Adam and Eve) was given the opportunity and ability to choose to rebel against him, and did so. Evil is a distortion of God's good creation. In essence, it is the rebellion of the creature against its Creator. That being so, there is hope. Surely the sovereign Creator is able to overcome the rebellion and remove the distortion in his own time and way!

This view of evil stands in marked contrast to what is found in some other religions. Some do make evil co-equal and co-eternal with God or the gods. This seems to have been the case with the religions of Mesopotamia and Canaan, which attributed what we would call 'evil' to the acts of the gods themselves. Some of the gods were seen as essentially evil – the bringers of famine, plague and so on. Other religions, like Platonism, see evil as eternal and an essential part of the material world. These are pessimistic views, because they imply that there can be no ultimate removal of evil and triumph of good. Some of the eastern religions and New Age philosophies that are gaining popularity in the West today regard evil as ultimately an illusion, a result of our frustrated desires. If we can learn to live free from desire, we will realize that neither good nor evil exists. Most of us would think that an unrealistic view. The Bible is thoroughly realistic. Evil is real and God hates it. It devastates his world. But the Bible is also optimistic in the long run. God is at work dealing with evil, and one day he will remove it completely.

Human nature

The Babylonian creation accounts agree with Genesis that humans are different from other creatures. We are *a mixture of the earthly and the heavenly*. In the *Atrahasis Epic* one of the gods is killed and his blood is mixed with clay to create humans. According to Genesis 1 – 3 we are on one level no different from the animals, made out of the dust of the earth. It is therefore not surprising that there is little difference between the basic biochemistry of the cells that make up our bodies and the cells of other animals, even the humble yeast cell. Nor should we be disturbed by the fact that we have other resemblances to the animals – in our instincts, behaviour patterns and so on.

Where some people go wrong is to assume that this animal-likeness is *all* that there is to be said about humans. This assumption often arises because of a failure to recognize the limitations of science. Genesis teaches, and our experience bears it out, that there is another level or aspect to human nature. This is our spiritual nature. We alone of the created beings are said to *bear God's image and likeness* (1:26–27). What does this mean? Scholars have debated this question long and often, and are not fully agreed as to the exact answer. Some have tried to make a distinction between 'image' and 'likeness'. This is probably not valid; in Genesis 5:1–3 the two terms seem to be used interchangeably. Also, the doubling up of similar terms like this is a common feature of Hebrew literature, especially poetry. It is generally agreed that attempts to define the 'image' in terms of one particular human quality (e.g. reason, moral sense, love) are mistaken. It is wider than that. We do best to think of it in terms of being made in such a way that we can reflect something of God's nature in our personality. The fact that we are made in this way prepares for the amazing event of the coming of Christ – of God the Son becoming a man. He was the perfect human image of God (2 Corinthians 4:4; Colossians 1:15).

Because we bear the image of God we are *God's representatives on earth*, and are given the authority to rule it on his behalf (Genesis 1:26–28). The point is sometimes made that in the Ancient Near East a conqueror of a city, when he left and went back home, would usually leave behind a statue of himself, sometimes with his laws inscribed on it, as a reminder of his authority over that city. One such statue, found in Syria, is described as the 'image and likeness' of the ruler. In the light of that, we can speak of humans as the symbols of God's rule and authority over the earth. Perhaps one reason for the prohibition in the Ten Commandments against making images of God is that not only does image-making limit and distort our view of God, but it also overlooks that humans are the only images of God allowed on earth! This is a very different valuation of humans than that of the Babylonians. Their creation stories say that we were created to be the slaves of the gods, providing them with their food and drink (through sacrifices) and building houses (temples) for them.

All views which see people as a means to an end, rather than as of value in themselves, fall short of the biblical valuation of human beings. This could be said of some modern political ideologies, such as Fascism and Marxism, which tend to treat the ordinary person simply as a means to achieving a political Utopia.

Humans were created by God *as sexual beings*, as men and women. In Genesis 1:27 the creation of humans as 'male and female' is closely related to the image of God. Since God is not a physical being, it cannot be the case that we reflect him simply in our sexuality. We may, however, have here a hint of the 'communal' nature of God which is represented in the doctrine of the Trinity. God's 'personality' is of a different, more complex, order than ours. It is better represented by the picture (image) of humans living together in loving, harmonious relationship than by that of an isolated individual human personality. In saying this, we must remember what was said in chapter 2 about doctrines as models or pictures, and not take the picture literally.

Genesis 2:18–24 says more about our sexuality than does Genesis 1:26–27. Because of the tendency to regard bodily desires as evil, some Christians have had a negative view of sex, especially its physical expression. But here we are clearly told that sex was God's idea! He thought it good that there should be men and women and that they should 'become one flesh', the biblical expression for sexual intercourse. But, and this is very important, the creator of sex has also told us the right way in which it should be expressed and enjoyed. This is within the relationship of life-long, single-partner marriage with a member of the opposite sex. This is the clear teaching of Genesis 2:24, to which Jesus appealed in his teaching (Mark 10:6–9): 'For this reason a man will leave his father and mother and be united to his wife, and they will become one flesh.'

Genesis 2:18 is sometimes, wrongly, taken to imply that women are inferior to men, simply their 'helpers': 'The LORD God said, "It is not good for the man to be alone. I will make a helper suitable for him."' In fact, the Hebrew word used here ('*ēzer*) is most often used of God when he helps his people (e.g. 1 Samuel 7:12). It hardly implies inferiority! On the contrary, woman is described as a suitable partner for man in the task of caring for God's world. *Men and women are different, but truly complementary* in that they 'complete' one another, the one making up for what the other lacks. The essential equality of men and women is beautifully expressed in the story of

Eve's creation, whether or not we take it literally. It speaks of woman being made of the same substance as man. Unlike the animals, she is not made out of a separate dust heap but from Adam's own body. It is probably significant that she is made from his rib. As it has been said: not from his head, to rule over him, or from his feet, to be trodden on by him, but from his side, to be his equal.

As we have seen, Genesis 1:26–28 gives to men and women the authority to 'subdue' and 'rule' the world. Some have seen this as a charter for the selfish exploitation of the earth. However, this authority must be seen in the context of men and women bearing God's image. We are expected to rule the world in God's place, as he would rule it. This means that we will not want to despoil what he saw as 'very good' when he had completed it. Our treatment of the world should reflect his wisdom and justice in the way we develop its resources and share them out among ourselves.

Finally, Genesis teaches that *we are worshipping beings.* This is shown by God blessing the seventh day and making it holy. We are made to live in a loving relationship with our Creator and need to put aside time to develop this through prayer, meditation on God's Word and worship. To some extent this is to be done individually but, because we are social creatures, it is also to be done in fellowship with other people. In his wisdom, God gave us the pattern of setting aside one day in seven to rest from work and from the other concerns that take up much of our time, and to spend time deepening our relationship with him.

Augustine of Hippo expressed the need that we have for a relationship with God when he said, 'Lord you made us for yourself, and we are restless until we find our rest in you.' When people ignore or reject God, that restlessness leads them to worship other 'gods', such as money, pleasure and power.

Fallen human nature

It is right that creatures should recognize and respect their Creator. But God wants such recognition and respect to be given freely by men and women. This is why he gave Adam and Eve the test regarding the tree of the knowledge of good and evil. He gave them the opportunity to decide whether or not to live in obedience to him.

It is not absolutely clear what that tree represents. Some limit it to moral knowledge, but a Hebrew phrase like this, stating two opposites, can be taken to mean 'everything'. Perhaps the right way to understand the test is to see it as meaning that the human search for knowledge of all kinds should be carried out in dependence on God and in the light of his revelation. We are not to grab knowledge purely for our own selfish ends.

Whatever the exact nature of the test, Adam and Eve failed. They gave in to the temptation to be like God in a wrong sense, to be his rivals instead of his representatives, and so became sinners. The effect of that sin is pictured in what follows. It can be seen in terms of four disrupted relationships.

• Most importantly, the relationship between us and our Creator has been affected. Instead of free and intimate friendship, there is fear and a shrinking from his presence (3:8–10).

• We are no longer at peace with ourselves. We have a sense of unease and shame (2:25; 3:7).

• We can no longer get on with each other. We start blaming other people for what goes wrong (3:12). What should have been the deepest and happiest relationship becomes a place of strife and exploitation (3:16).

• Our relationship with nature becomes a source of frustration, so that we seem always to be battling with it (3:17–19).

Here in this simple story is a powerful presentation of the spiritual source of our psychological, social and environmental problems. They all flow from the loss of a right relationship with our Creator God.

In Genesis 4 – 6 we see the effects of sin spreading out like the ripples from a stone thrown into a pond. The murderous jealousy of Cain, the vengefulness of Lamech and the sexual immorality of 'the sons of God', build up to the widespread evil in the generation of Noah. At that point God steps in to demonstrate that he will not tolerate the uninhibited spread of evil.

Yet, in this dark picture, there are chinks of light. We are told that the image of God had not been removed from humans. Adam and Eve pass it on to their children (5:1–3). The image may be marred and distorted, but it is not totally destroyed. It is still possible to live in a right relationship with God, as Enoch did (5:21–24). Had the image been lost completely, we would not be human any more but simply complex animals. The fact that we remain in God's image gives us some ground for hope. God has not given up on his purpose for his creation.

Salvation

This brings us to the subject of God's plan of salvation. Alongside each of God's acts of punishment of sin in Genesis 1 – 11 goes a gracious act of mercy. This is most obvious in the case of the flood. In this case, not only does God save Noah and his family but, at the end of the flood, he makes a covenant with all creation not to carry out a similar widespread punishment of sin whilst this world-order remains. It is there also in the case of Cain. He is doomed to be a restless wanderer, but in answer to his own plea he is given a mark to protect his life. Similarly, when Adam and Eve are driven out of Eden, God himself clothes them. Here we have hints that it is not God's intention to wipe out his creation that has fallen into sin, but to limit the effects of that sin and maybe to do more than that. But how will he do it?

Genesis 1 – 11 is the prologue to the Bible, so it does not answer that question fully, but it does indicate where the answer will lie. When the serpent is cursed, there is a promise that the offspring of the woman will one day crush the head of the serpent – that is, destroy the source of evil (3:15). How this will come about begins to unfold after the incident of the Tower of Babel. At first this seems to be the one act of punishment for sin in Genesis 1 – 11 which lacks any corresponding act of grace. This is because the act of grace is actually recorded in Genesis 12:1–3. At Babel humankind was confused and scattered by God. Now we are told of how God called a man to become the father of a nation through which all the scattered nations would be blessed.

So the story that leads through the great men and women of faith to Jesus the Saviour begins to unfold and, through him, leads on to the new heaven and the new earth – where the redeemed of humanity from every nation and language group live, once again, in the immediate presence of God and have access to the tree of life.

Further reading

D. Atkinson, *The Message of Genesis 1 – 11*, The Bible

Speaks Today (Leicester and Downers Grove, IL: IVP, 1980). An excellent exposition of these chapters.

H. Blocher, *In the Beginning* (Leicester and Downers Grove, IL: IVP, 1984). A detailed study of Genesis 1 – 3.

D. Kidner, *Genesis*, Tyndale Old Testament Commentary (London: Tyndale Press, 1967). A good, short commentary.

G. J. Wenham, *Genesis 1 – 15*, Word Biblical Commentary (Waco, Texas: 1987). A very good detailed commentary.

10

Genesis and science today

As we have looked at ideas about the relationship of science to Genesis, you may have been surprised by the variety of views and lack of conclusive answers. You need not be. Our understanding of anything, including the Bible, is never perfect. What is more, as we saw in chapter 2, science is always only an approximation to ultimate reality. If our interpretation of the Bible agreed perfectly with the modern science of today, it almost certainly would not agree with the modern science of tomorrow! The really important thing is that we should understand exactly what Genesis teaches.

In the opening chapters of this book we saw that science provides only one limited way of looking at the world – in terms of its *mechanism*. Christianity, we argued, provides a different but complementary view – concerned with the *meaning* of life in this world. We would expect the Bible, the source-book of Christian teaching, to be primarily concerned with questions of meaning rather than mechanism. This turns out to be the case for Genesis 1 – 11, especially if we read these chapters according to the literary-cultural approach, which seems to me to be the right approach. For example, we saw that although Genesis 1 – 3 teaches that God created human beings it does not rule out the possibility that he did so through an evolutionary process. Whether he did or not is a question which it is proper for science to investigate.

Although the Bible leaves very many questions like this wide open for scientific study, there are two ways in which it sometimes comes into direct contact with science.

Revelation and history

In the Bible God reveals to us the spiritual truth he wants us to know. Some of that revelation comes through accounts of things that God has done in the course of world history. It is right and proper for us to ask whether historians and scientists can find any evidence concerning these events or throw any other light on them – and to take seriously the answers they give as another way of discovering the truth which ultimately has its source in God. We asked these kinds of questions about the flood. The historical and scientific evidence suggested that it was a major catastrophe in the history of the Near East but was probably not a world-wide one. Such an understanding of it does not conflict with the way the story is told in Genesis 6 – 9. If it did, we would have to ask the historians and scientists to re-examine their conclusions or look for more evidence because we would expect that ultimately their conclusions would be compatible with the biblical account.

When appealing to scientific and historical evidence we have to be careful, for two reasons. The first is the nature of biblical language. If it is symbolic language, or some other kind of figurative language, it may not be easy to relate what is said to scientific or historical evidence. Secondly, God is free to do miracles which do not fit into the normal course of history or the laws of nature. However, it is unwise to appeal to miracles to explain things – as some do, for example, with aspects of the flood – when the Bible does not speak of God doing miracles.

A way of seeing things

In chapter 2, the Christian way of understanding reality was compared to an artist's impression of a building, and the scientific view was compared to one of the architect's plans. This indicates another, more far-reaching way in which the Bible can interact with science. For the Christian, scientific truth has to be seen within the framework provided by the distinctive view of reality which results from accepting the teaching of the Bible.

Genesis 1 – 11 is a very important section of the Bible because these chapters contribute a great deal to the formation of an overall view of reality. We have seen what these chapters teach about such fundamental matters as the nature of God, the nature of the world, what it means to be human, evil and salvation. All of this has implications which the Christian must take seriously in relation to science.

Science, God and creation

Genesis 1 teaches that we live in a universe created by God. Science can neither prove nor disprove this. At most, scientists may be able to tell us the processes which God used to bring into being the universe as we know it. Even if it is true that the universe developed from a 'quantum vacuum', according to well-known physical laws, that does not make God unnecessary. We are still left asking, 'Why should there be a quantum vacuum with the potential to produce a universe?' The unbeliever may reply that it is just 'the way things are'. It is at least as rational to reply that there is a God who created the quantum vacuum, and that the physical laws are God at work shaping his creation. In chapter 1 we saw that it was this Christian view of the universe which formed the basis of modern science and that, without it, it is difficult to find a rational basis for science.

Science and spirituality

Because something of God's power and nature can be seen in what God has created (Romans 1:20), people have often had a sense of the presence of God when closely in touch with that creation. This has sometimes brought people to faith in God. A scientist I know dates the beginning of his spiritual journey to watching the sun rise when he was on a biology field-trip on the South Downs of England. Awe-struck by the beauty of the scene, he had a deep sense of God's presence. Not having had any interest in religion before, he decided to go to a church to find out about this God who had met him in the countryside.

Numerous Christians who work in science can testify to the fact that their study of God's creation nourishes their faith. One of the deepest religious experiences I have had happened in the Radcliffe Science Library in Oxford. As I spent a morning studying the chemistry and biochemistry of a vitamin called biotin, I became increasingly amazed at how each atom in that molecule contributed, both on its own, and also in conjunction with the others, to the function of that molecule in the living cell. When I put the books and journals aside at the end of the morning, I had a deep sense of awe. I rephrased the words of the psalmist (Psalm 19:1): the vitamins are telling the glory of God, and the living cell proclaims his handiwork.

Science and people

We have seen that Genesis teaches that we are made out of the dust of the ground, but also that we are made in the image of God. We are both earthly and heavenly, material and spiritual. Being bearers of God's image sets us apart from the animals, but being made out of the dust of the ground unites us with them.

It is right that in their quest to understand people better, scientists should sometimes study the human brain as if it were a computer or compare human behaviour with that of animals. However, Christians must protest when some then claim that we are *just* machines with no freewill, or *nothing but* complex animals. Such claims are contradicted by biblical teaching. They are also logically invalid, because they take one limited view of reality as the total picture. Scientists adopt such limited views as a way of isolating one aspect of a complicated thing (in this case a person) so that they can have something simple enough to study. But what is learnt in this way must then be fitted back into the bigger picture, not taken to be the whole picture. We want to say that Christian teaching sketches out an outline of that picture, which is then filled in with the help of knowledge from other sources.

Science and technology

According to Genesis 1 – 2, God gave humans *the responsibility of caring for his creation* and *the right to make use of it to meet their needs*. Belief in this responsibility and this right was one of the things which motivated the early scientists to study the world and develop technologies to make use of their discoveries for the benefit of the human race.

We have to face the fact that things have often gone wrong, sometimes terribly so. The right to use the world has been separated from the responsibility to care for it as God would have done. What was originally very good has been defaced and despoiled. This is, of course, a result of greed and selfishness – expressions of the fallenness of human nature. Christians should be in the forefront of those who protest at the damage being done to our environment, God's good creation, by the thoughtless or wrongly exploitative use of science and technology. We should be pressing for technology to be used in ways that are environmentally sound. Any unavoidable environmental damage should be counted as part of the cost of the technology, and it should be repaired as far as possible out of its profits.

Scientists: finite and fallen

Scientists are human beings. Like all of us they are both finite and fallen. Their finiteness means that their understanding of the universe is always incomplete. As a result, it is also sometimes mistaken, because some vital aspect of the truth is always missing.

Because they are fallen, the attitudes, motives and methods of scientists are sometimes wrong. Instead of seeking the truth for its own sake, a scientist may be more interested in his or her reputation. As a result, there may be a refusal to face up to evidence which challenges a pet theory, or even, in extreme cases, a falsification of results so that they fit the theory. A desire to get results at all costs may lead to a refusal to stop and ask awkward questions about the experimental methods being used, and an impatience with those who do – for example questions like 'Should animals be used in experiments and, if so, under what circumstances?' or 'Should experiments be carried out on tissue from aborted foetuses?'

The fallenness of men and women means that the powers which science and technology make available to us are sometimes used in harmful ways. The knowledge and skills which lead to genetically engineered bacteria which produce insulin to help diabetics can also be used to produce bacteria for germ warfare. Here is a challenge for scientists to get together with ethicists and other representatives of society to find ways of controlling the use of scientific discoveries and skills.

Science and salvation

The picture is not all black, of course. Far from it! Science and technology have done a great deal to benefit the human race, but there is now a more balanced assessment of their achievements than was the case half a century ago.

Early in the twentieth century, many thought and hoped that by education (especially in science), social welfare programmes (in which such sciences as medicine and nutrition would play a big part) and technology, the human race would finally reach a reasonable approximation to the ideal society – in a sense achieve its own 'salvation'. World wars (made more horrific by chemical and atomic weapons), corrupt politicians and bureaucrats, and the environmental damage caused by some technologies have dashed those hopes.

The Bible teaches that the only real way of salvation is to be found in accepting the good news of what God has done for us through Jesus Christ. His death and resurrection make it possible for us to receive God's forgiveness and the power of his Spirit. That power gradually restores his image in our personality, undoing the ravages of the fall. But the good news is not just about individual salvation. The restoration of our relationship with God and the image of God in us enables us to work at the restoration of the other relationships damaged by the fall – our social relationships and our relationship with nature – so as to make them as pleasing to God as we can.

This is *not* a matter of trying to achieve Utopia, heaven on earth, by our own efforts. It *is* a matter of joining battle with God against the evil that has entered his creation and despoiled it. The knowledge and power that science gives us can be used to aid us in this battle. But if it is to be used in this way it has to be understood within the framework of the Christian view of reality. As we have seen, Genesis 1 – 11, properly interpreted and understood, makes a major contribution to the formation of that view.

The most important things to gain from this book are not answers to the historical or scientific problems raised by Genesis 1 – 11. Those answers do have some value in helping us come to a better understanding of these chapters and a deeper confidence in them. However, it is more important to understand the message of these chapters and to let them shape our understanding of life. That will then help us to live in the way that God wants us to, as people made in his image and likeness.

Further reading

R. J. Berry (editor), *Real Science, Real Faith* (Eastbourne: Monarch, 1991). Sixteen scientists talk about their Christian faith.

Web-sites

The following web-sites are maintained by evangelical Christian organizations interested in relating their faith to modern science.

- Christians in Science: http://www.cis.org.uk/
- Christian Students in Science:
  http://www.csis.org.uk/
- American Scientific Affiliation:
  http://asa.calvin.edu/

Index of authors and subjects

191